Once there was a village
whose harvest came in
and it was poisonous.
Those who ate of it would become insane.

"There is but one thing to do," said the Elder
"We must eat the grain to survive,
but there must be those among us
who will remember that we are insane."

Anonymous

May we learn to see our community
as interwoven branches on a sacred Tree.

The key to shapeshifting our world is to transition
from "Us" and "Them", to "WE".

Quynn Red Mountain

Are you an Animist?

ANIMISM is a name for the life force that flows
through All That Is and connects all of us in the sacred web of life.

An ANIMIST is one who learns how to move with this flow
and sees self in all other beings (human and beyond).

ANIMISTS are spirit world travelers, artists, and Earth protectors
who form KINDREDS of Animist community.

May the sacred wisdom keepers guide your path.

LAND ACKNOWLEDGEMENT

I offer gratitude to the ancestors and spirits of the lands who have taught and nurtured me in this life, specifically the lands that are now called Portland, Oregon and Tucson, Arizona. These lands are the traditional home of the Multnomah, Clackamas, Chinook, and Willamette in the Portland area, and the Tohono O'odham in the Tucson area. It is important to recognize that all lands of Turtle Island belong to First Nations/Indigenous Peoples who have lived here since time immemorial.

I offer gratitude to each sacred place highlighted in the images of this guide book, all which I had the blessed opportunity to visit and learn from over the last 20+ years. Each mirrored image honors the depth of teaching I have received from the sacred lands of what are now called Oregon, Washington, Utah, Arizona and Idaho, all traditional lands of many Indigenous Peoples.

Dedication: Prayers of protection for all Indigenous Peoples of Earth who have kept the wisdom alive through horrific times.

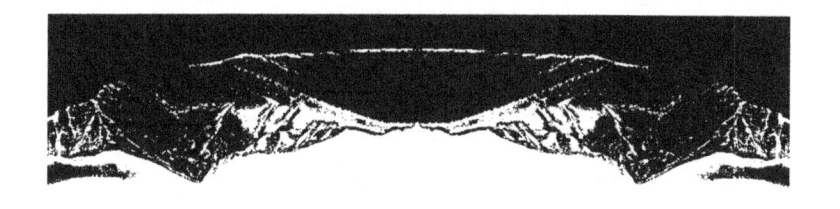

~WE~
THE BEGINNER'S FIELD GUIDE
TO FULL CIRCLE ANIMISM

ANIMISM=WE ARE ALL CONNECTED
IN THE SACRED WEB OF LIFE

BROUGHT TO YOU BY QUYNN RED MOUNTAIN

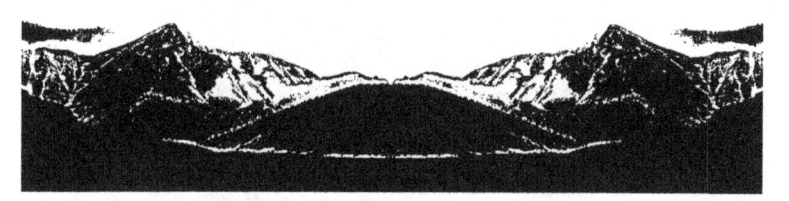

QUYNN'S GRATITUDES
I offer gratitude and honor for my Mother, Sue Ellen, and my father, George, as well as my Animist Ancestors who have always been there with me.

Help along the way: I am still doing this work because many people helped me, especially in the early years. I write the names of the Elders who housed, supported, fed and financed me and this work. I list them here (in order of appearance) to say thank you, and I ask for forgiveness for any misstep along the way. To those who have passed, I look forward to reconnecting again. Thank you to Burton, Walter, Tahlia, Ken, Peggy, Maria, Thomas, Jacob, Gayle, Linn, Ellie, Uncle Bill, Elisabeth, Steve and Dee.

Finally, big gratitude to all who have sat in circle with me over the last two decades. It is you who have kept me on this ever unfolding path.

Table of Contents

Welcome home-Forward for this next Edition…page 4

Chapter 1: OLD WAYS NEW AGAIN…page 9
Chapter 2: CONNECTING WITHIN…page 31
Chapter 3: HEALING FOR OUR PAST…page 56
Chapter 4: SACRED PLACE…page 75
Chapter 5: GETTING ANSWERS…page 94
Chapter 6: RHYTHMS, FEATHER, SMOKE…page 112
End=RESTORING ANIMIST TIMELINES…page 137

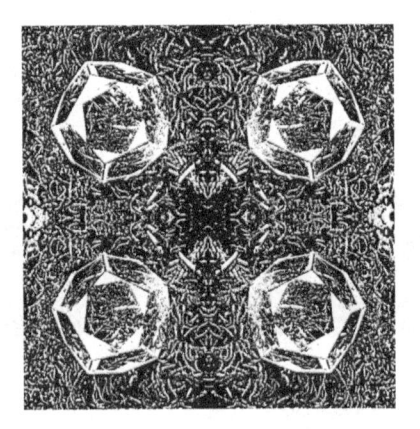

May your crystalline nature be blessed 5 times

1st edition 2004- 2nd edition 2013- 3rd edition 2021
© Quynn Red Mountain
Thanks Merrie, Steve and Caitlin for editing help on all editions!

Paperback B&W Mirrored Photograph Sketches (sketch photo),
Blessings and Poems by Quynn Red Mountain.
Color Mirror Photos are in the Kindle version &
in the forthcoming Sacred Nature Portals Oracle deck.

Forward to this 3rd Edition

Welcome. My name is Quynn Red Mountain and the stories and ideas on the following pages have come through me during my life so far. The messages, tales, journeys and practices have been shared with me as inspiration, voice, vision and imagination in both day and night dreams. They have been persistent and determined that I bring it all into this world at this time.

The visions, prophecies (not shared in this book) and foretellings have been consistent, never wavering, and the message has been clear. It is time for these ideas, and I must share them with you. I tell you this because there is a voice in my head that says "that is ridiculous. Who are you to do this? Why you? You aren't special." Maybe so. However, over a couple decades of living with these messages I know that the guidance doesn't wrongly guide me. Things have played out and have come to be. So, I have enough inner "proof" that I must do what is wanted of me, to share this body of work with you. Consider it a map, a key, a field guide to help you find your way, in your own way. You are important here.

I hope that you, the reader and seeker, find guidance, trail markers and affirmation in these stories for your inner journeys of healing, and your adventures in reconnecting with the living world of Full Circle Animism. Many blessings for your travels. I look forward to crossing paths with you.

I do not speak for any Animist or Shamanic Practitioners, nor anyone of any tradition. I do speak for the voices I hear and for that which I call "Full Circle" Animism (not Animism in general). I share my experiences and research to assist in the collective healing. This guide is for all who seek to dismantle colonization, reclaim their inner world and express their sacred self in our beautiful web of life.

Words in this field guide might make you uncomfortable. If so, work with the feeling in the exercises and journeys. Don't stop, keep going.

As always, use what is helpful, leave the rest. Maybe it is helpful now, maybe later.

A TRIBE OF ONE BECOMES KINDRED & COMES FULL CIRCLE ~The origin story and evolution of this book~

In September of 1995, when I was 28 years old, I had a logically unexplainable experience resulting in a head injury (see my "Ghost Story" at https://quynn.com/quynn-red-mountain/the-calling/), which initiated me into the lifelong adventure of hearing voices, receiving visions, dreams and "downloads", which have guided me through each step as this new path emerged in my life.

During the summer of 1999, I was in Moab, Utah hiking around many rock cliffs and canyons. One day, I was led on a long hike under a strong sun which created an altered state. After hours of walking, I came to a cliff and when I looked over the edge, I was shocked to see that the red rocks and shadows below shape shifted into an ancient face of a human grandfather. After a moment, I began hearing a voice in my head as the wind filled my ears. What he told me now seems obvious, but at the time it was an "ah-hah" moment. I heard his voice in my head say, "At one point in history, everyone, no matter where your ancestors came from, knew the ways of 'magic' and knew how to live with the Earth. You have these ancestors inside you, in your DNA, and you can call on them and ask them to whisper to you. They can tell you what to do in these times." This message changed me, and it became a foundation of my studies, teachings and ministry. "It" is in all of us.

In the summer of 2001, I was upset because I was not finding other humans who were like-minded enough to call them "my Tribe" (the word I used back then). "Where are they?!" I pleaded again and again. One day a voice came into my head and stopped me in my tracks. It said, "Quynn, you are a "Tribe" of One. Since this is so, what does your "Tribe" look like? How do you pray? What do you believe? It is time for you to find out. Once you do this, you will begin to find others who are kindred spirits."

These two messages became the inspirations for the book I began to write in 2002, at the age of 35, which I called "A Tribe of One." In 2013 I updated some of the content for a 2nd edition. The field guide you are reading now has been re-named and re-edited in 2020-21, during the time of Covid-19, the much overdue Racial Reckoning, and the obvious emergence of the oncoming Climate Emergency. This 3rd edition bears yet a new name, simple and clear, The Beginner's Field

Guide to Full Circle Animism, released in 2021, just in time for all that is coming.

I changed the title of this book for a deeply personal reason. When the voice told me way back then that I was a "Tribe of One," I took that message to heart. The next 20 years of my life and work addressed the questions the voice asked me, "How does your Tribe pray?" and "What does your Tribe believe?" I am grateful to say that I have answered those questions to my own satisfaction. I now live by them and share them with others. My entire body of work to this point has teased apart these questions to offer techniques and practices that anyone can use to explore their own soul healing and Animist homecoming after generations of trauma and forgetting. Once we understand that we each have Animist heritage and find ways to heal our Animist selves as individuals, we can begin our initiation of becoming kindred with the living world around and within us. This is our sacred task.

At the beginning of this new era, I am 53 years old. As a female, white bodied human, I see and understand so much more than what I was able to see and understand in my younger years and earlier times. This guide, including the title, has been updated to reflect what is needed now, to implement and model the ways in which we create an authentic spiritual practice from the ashes of our colonized minds and to fully understand how feeding justice (social, gender, racial, climate +) is the spirituality that will lead us where we need to be, together.

I have written this book for anyone who's Animist ancestral connection has been forgotten, wounded, atrophied and/or severed due to colonization, and is now called to remember how to heal their connections. As healing occurs, a personally authentic, culturally non-appropriative and ancestrally focused practice can emerge.
The diverse and beautiful original way of humanity has not gone anywhere, it is right here waiting…for YOU. I call us Full Circle Animists.

If you find the words that follow disturbing, please understand that no offense is intended, simply breathe and let them sink in. Your ancestral line has survived to date because they hid their Animist ways, even from themselves, so give yourself time to decide how you feel about it all. However, it is also important to say that your uncomfortable feelings (or mine!) do not necessarily make these words untrue. Trauma from the past is in all of us. May Peace be felt by all beings. May Peace begin with me.

In Full Circle Animism, Kindred means:
A person's relatives in the Web of Life; kinfolk; kin. A group of persons (human and other-than-human) related to another by birth, descent, marriage or belief; kindred spirits.

In Full Circle Animism, Colonized means:
The worldwide practice of an imperial nation conquering a place and its Indigenous population. Over time, colonizer language and cultural values are forced upon the People causing generational trauma. These toxic values are often internalized by those who have been colonized, and colonizers poison the land, air and water in the process.

To dive deeper, explore the Restoring your Animist Heart course
weboflifeanimists.com/product/restoring-your-animist-heart-course/
See coupon code in last pages.

May the rattles of knowing guide you within.

Do you remember?
Do you remember the time
when we danced because the Earth called?
No need to speak the same language
because the rhythms spoke for us all.

Our ancestral connections guide travels
to places forever in our minds
To gather healing medicine for ourselves and our allies.

"Where did these times go?" you ask,
I have wondered this myself
and as I continue to practice love,
I find them hiding on a dusty old mind-shelf.

We may feel alone,
And we may look around and see pain,
yet when we dance and trance together
we breathe life to the dream once again.

A Note to Begin…
The content of this field guide is offered as a healing and activating toolbox filled with possibilities. It is important to mention that oftentimes our healing and activations emerge from discomfort and challenge, as they can promote growth and evolution. My request is that when you feel any resistance, anger or sadness from reading any of my words, I ask you to sit with it and address the emotion in the exercises provided. Use the feelings as fuel for your inner exploration, healing and understanding of your authentic self, as well as an illumination of the ways in which you have been colonized, trained and restrained by the culture in which you were raised.

Also, of course, the words I use in this book are my words. Part of this process is for you to find your own ways and words. So, when you disagree or question the way I describe something, you are invited to listen for your own. This is the purpose of the stories shared. Thank you for your interest. Many blessings. We All Belong.

May the stone Goddesses protect you always.

Chapter 1:
OLD WAYS BECOME NEW AGAIN

That which we call "History" shows that belief systems come and go over time. Animism is often described as the oldest and most consistent human way of being (sometimes considered a "life-way" or "religion" in modern cultures). This multifaceted way of life guides every original Earth culture in their own way, and at one point all human cultures were, what we now call, Animist. The simplest description is that the breath of Spirit moves in all and all beings are connected in the web of life. It is time to reclaim many of our discarded, destroyed and buried Animistic ways of the past, for the good that they contained, so we can collectively co-create the world that wants to emerge. These ways honor the Earth and the diversity of life, which you and I are a part.

In colonized culture(s), children learn about the past from the oppressor's point of view. This colonizing spell is now broken so a growing number of Animist people are actively reclaiming oppressed cultural stories and healing the traumas from colonization. Collectively, we are in a time of the Great Remembering of our troubling past, while calling upon wise truths that reconnect us to ourselves and each other on this sacred Mother planet we call Earth.

If you have come this far in your life and this book, you have a sense that our human culture is playing out a disturbing story that has been thrust upon all of us, while a few humans are wholeheartedly enraptured within it. The story of monotheist, white, male, and human supremacy has spread across the Earth and made land barren, people selfish, and sickness strong. Its followers are told that they are above all others and that the world will end. They will get to leave this place to go to *their* "heaven." For over a thousand years, this story was forced upon more and more of the Peoples that inhabit this beautiful Earth, and today all have been traumatized by it. Many who have been colonized still perpetuate the traumas upon others. The time is NOW to have accountability, justice, and healing of past pains so we can attend to needed actions that can help us weave through this time with grace.

How did we get here?
Humans can be limited in our belief systems. Individuals and communities have always created fights out of fear and greed, waging wars upon one another because of "values" regarding "us" and "them". Throughout time, Animist communities have had names for themselves, that when translated to English, meant something like "the true People," or "the real People."
This meant that some other groups of people were though to be not as "true" or "real" as them, instead considered "other."

Until recent times, Earth had a remedy for this. For many thousands of years people lived in groups separated by valleys and seas and mountains. Some of these groups got along and some did not. If a group encountered an undesirable group, they would go to "war" to keep the "undesirables" away from their people, their land and their food. The point of these wars was not to convert the "others" to their way of thinking, nor was the point always to completely wipe out the other group. Sometimes, their concept of war was to take valuables, or to get the others away from them and show their strength as a People.

At specific points in the past, groups emerged with belief systems that they were the "chosen" People, and that they had dominion over anyone contrary to their way of thinking and living. These monotheists (one true God) moved across the "old world" with violence and a belief system that said, "Convert or die." Then, the evolution of colonization dumped sickness and the myth of their supremacy on the Earth honoring kindred around the world.

OUR UNFORTUNATE RECENT PAST

Everyone can agree that it is uncomfortable remembering painful parts of our personal and collective history. Many say, or hear, "The past is the past! Forget it and move on!". However, until and unless we examine the patterns of domination and mean spiritedness of many who have gone before us, and that still lives within the human family, we shall never be able to be free.

There has been much trauma experienced by people in Animist cultures all over the world, at the hands of invader tribes with superior technology and a belief of superiority. This is not to say that Animists don't go to "war" amongst tribes, clans or nations. Throughout time war has been waged between Animist tribes to revenge a wrong, defend or take territory, train brave warriors, and to choose their leaders. Speaking specifically about the historic triangle of Europe, Africa and the "Americas" in the last 1500 years, religious monotheists decided that they were the conquerers for their one true God. They used their powers of disease and weapon to overpower Animist people and take the lands of these continents. The people who felt (and still feel) superior wielded their power over younger generations to convince or coerce them to think that their old ways were evil.

Unfortunately, there are many remaining accounts of this practice, in just one example of what is commonly called "Latin America", one can read the conquistadors' own accounts of why and how they achieved these takeovers, we see that their original reason for the religious domination and torture was often the church's desire to take the wealth of the People. This, they have effectively achieved.

TRIGGER WARNING~ Some readers might feel uncomfortable about hearing such truthful stories, but we must honestly remember our history, to free ourselves in our present. To illustrate this point, we offer the example of one Animist culture. Entire continents were completely devastated by contact with those we now call colonizers, who stole all the resources they could, in the name of their god.

GOLD, GLORY AND GOSPEL

"The Funnel of Gold" by Mendel Peterson (1975) is just one book of many that compiles the history of the Spanish treasure fleets as they dominated the "new world", and realized how much there was to take back to Spain and Portugal. They brought with them the conquistadors' version of Christianity.

"When Christ became King of the Earth, all heathen peoples lost title to their possessions. Peter, the Apostle, inherited Christ's dominion over the Earth, and the Popes inherited it from Peter." A fourteenth-century papal authority, Heinreich Suso (page 6 of "The Funnel of Gold")

"The pattern of exploitation was pretty much the same whether it was Hispaniola, Cuba, Panama, Mexico or Peru. First, the invading Spaniards looted the natives of any gold or silver they might possess, killing them if necessary. Then the graves and temples were systematically stripped of any precious offerings or ornament. In the process of conquest, the population of the country was decimated, and the native leaders killed; even the unresisting ones were often put to the sword. After the country was subjugated, the remaining Indians, in the name of Christian education, were apportioned out to the Spanish soldiers according to the rank of the soldier and were then forced to work the placed deposits of gold. Many of them were literally worked to death. The last stage consisted of locating and mining the lodes which fed the placer deposits. Here the natives suffered most. Accustomed to living free lives, they died by the thousands in the mines." (page 34)

Such methods, while varying to some degree, have been implemented in many places, and times, around this Earth. Historical examples include the first "take-over" of the Animist tribes of what we now call "Europe" by invaders with a cross, then the crusades, the Spanish inquisition, the African holocaust (slave-trade), the hostile take-over and genocide of the entire "Americas" from north to south, as well as any other place they deemed desirable. This is the history of most Earthlings, and it is likely a part of your history. There are too many other similar stories, all over the world. What is most important is that all who are trying to break free from an oppressive past, not then become oppressors when the chance arises.

The good news now is that many of us are being asked to remember how to be in relationship with human and non-human kin on our beautiful planet Earth. Many are remembering the soul pains of our collective past so we can lay down the remnants of colonized mind. We ask our Animist ancestors to help us heal our wounds so we can emerge into a reality of cooperation and equality. It *is* possible, and it is our work to create it.

Where do we go from here?

I invite you to look within yourself. My hope is that the stories in this book might enhance your necessary journey of personal healing and reconnection to the sacred web of life. The time of Covid has begun, what my guiding allies have long called, the "After Times." For better and worse, we are at the edge of so much change that is inevitable, and so it is a perfect time for you to do this inner work so that you are ready for what comes.

How do we walk away from one belief and breathe life into another?

We change our world by:
- Liberating ourselves from our own colonized minds
- Reconnecting with our ancestors and allies within/around us
- Tending the wounds of personal and ancestral trauma
- Sharing needed mutual aid with others
- Working as a Kindred to change the structures of oppression
- Remembering and creating structures that support nourishment for the peoples of Earth

No matter which paths we collectively choose, we can each decide to be a person who is:
- Connected with the web of life
- Committed to justice for Earth and her peoples
- A living example of Animistic ways

The stories and exercises that follow are hints to help you see the ways you are chaining yourself to the world that has been created for you in the hopes that you can then liberate yourself through your own discoveries and truths. If there is one thing that our colonized minds are beginning to remember, it is that "reality" is much more than we have been taught.

*May the ancient Cedar trees
create portals of possibility for you.*

ANIMISM AS SPIRITUAL PRACTICE

An Animist is one who is connected to all life, as well as multiple layers of reality. This natural ability is enhanced by honing the senses, learning to quiet the mind and creating a sacred environment within. Here you will not learn rituals, tools, or practices from any one group of Animist people. There are thousands of Kindreds in the present, and even more in the past, that honor Animism in a variety of ways. Since many of us are remembering our connection and creating new pathways for our time, this study focuses on budding our Animist roots that can support future expansion.

RESPECTING SHAMANIC CULTURE

Many anthropologists (generally white Christian men) in the past used the word "Animist" to describe Indigenous peoples around the globe in a demeaning way, similar to "heathen." In the late 20th century, white metaphysical people began to use the word "Shamanism" to describe Animist peoples around the world. These words are not necessarily interchangeable.

*All Shamanic cultures are Animist.
Not all Animist cultures are Shamanic.*

The word "Shaman" comes from a Siberian Evenk and Manchu word šaman to describe a very specific role, as well as a set of beliefs and practices. Other people are more qualified to describe Shamanic culture, so two resources are listed below:

1) "Called by the Spirits" by Buryat Shamaness Sarangerel Odigan
2) A facebook group- 3 Worlds Shamanism – which hosts an extensive library of information www.facebook.com/groups/3worldsshamanism

To offer respect to the peoples of Shamanic cultures, and all the atrocities they have faced, I have chosen to only use the words Animism, Animist practitioner, and Animist, when describing the spiritual work in this field guide. It is important that as we move forward together, we use the word Shaman respectfully and appropriately, only when referring to the specific culture of Shamanic peoples and not to describe Animism as a whole.

Today, many colonized people believe that the world of Animism is not accessible to them anymore and that Animistic beliefs only belong to mysterious people in faraway lands. This may leave these seekers feeling that they have no direct access for themselves. Fortunately, this veil of forgetting is beginning to lift as colonized people remember that we all belong in the beautiful web of life.

ANIMISM BELONGS TO ALL

All people of the Earth, at one time, were Animist people, although they would not have called themselves such a word. They would have simply said they lived in the ways they had always lived. In every branch of your tall family tree, your kinfolk were Earth and Moon honoring peoples. Know that before they were colonized, all your ancestors were Nature people: often called a version of Pagans, Heathens, or Witches by the ones who ended up dominating them. These ancestors flourished long before any of the religions called Christianity, Judaism, Islam, Hindu, or Buddhism began.

You are a part of the Animist renaissance in the modern age. You decolonize your soul by listening for the wise teachings that you hear on the breeze in your mind. You can hear the guides and allies around you when you quiet yourself and listen. This takes practice, but if you are willing, you will hear. What you do with the heard guidance is up to you. If you do not heed it, what happens is up to you.

May the foods of this Earth bless you with health.

MYTHS OF OUR TIME

What is a myth? The *Merriam-Webster Dictionary* says a myth is: "A traditional story of historical events that serves to unfold part of the world view of a people or explain a practice, belief, or natural phenomenon." For any story to become a myth, it must be told over and over. Myths are created from tales of extraordinary events in extraordinary times. We are now living in such mythmaking times. As we live our lives, we are creating the stories of our experience that will be told over and over throughout the generations. Our multifaceted story of Now is being created, and lived, by all of us together.

As individuals, we are each an amazing and unique creation who has never existed before. Similarly, as a world human culture, we are living in a time of "Never Before." There have been many times in the past that have had mythmaking qualities, and today we are swimming in a sea of chemicals, technologies and sickness that have never existed before in human history. Each new element brings profound effects on individuals as well as human and non-human cultures. While the details of these shifts are yet unknown, there are ancient practices and stories of wisdom that can help us navigate through the "Sea of Never Before."

What stories will be created from our times, to be told forever more? Have we created a dystopian tale of who we are? Myths, like prophecies, *can* be changed. If you do not find current colonized cultural stories helpful, then what is *your* story? Some assume that myths were only made in ancient times, but our cultural stories must continue to be created by our experiences, and then told to others. We are the creators of our myths, by telling our stories, over and over, until they become the guiding and helpful myths for generations to come.

YOU BELONG

For the health of Earth's people, plants, elements and animals, as well as the planet itself, it is important for you to unlock your inner communication skills. It is time to remember the Animist wisdom that is buried within you, and create the new traditions of balance and magic, today, and for the times to come. The words written here are intended to help you understand your Animist heritage, feel closer to the natural world around you and learn ways to communicate more clearly with your inner guidance. You have a birthright to reclaim. The world needs you to remember.

Wind and Water
Stone and Stream
Ancestors calling to us
from the Dream.
"Remember," they whisper,
to the cells of our souls
"Remember the secrets of Creatrix and Crone."
So we call to you Butterfly,
Snake, Coyote and Bat.
Honeybee, Fish, Beaver, Bison and Bobcat.
Help us old wise ones of wing, fur and fin.
We know you can help us remember our Kin.
Those who knew how you speak,
and who heard their own voices within.

So we ask in prayerful voices,
because our people have strayed,
we ask that you forgive us,
and help us remember your ways.

YOU ARE WHOLE

Many people have feelings or memories from the past that cause pain. All of us live in a culture that causes pain on many levels. If you receive nothing else from these stories, know that you must keep seeking. There *is* something else. *You are not alone.*

Your journey of healing and reconnection will take everything you have, but you will succeed because the web of life is calling to you, it wants to help you. Your prize is confidence in your sanity and peace of mind that no one can disturb. The cost of this wonderful gift is this: when you feel centered, and even when you do not, find and create ways to give back and pay it forward.

May the powers of the drum, mica,
wing and antler be with you.

SPIRIT WORLD CONNECTION

Remembering how to identify and trust benevolent aspects of the non-physical (inner/spirit) world is an intricate practice. Many have been taught that to communicate with the realms of Spirit is weird, dangerous or demon work. However, we must remember that other realms do exist, they are a part of our "reality". Often our inner world speaks to us in symbols, patterns and code. It is a deep blessing to remember how to listen within so that you can decipher the messages that are coming to you, and make any changes needed. You are built for these connections and this wisdom is within you.

An important thing to remember when learning from the inner realms is discernment. How do you trust the information given? How do you know the "NOW" moment in which to act or not act? How do you keep the ego in check? How do you know what is being transmitted is "real" and helpful? Each seeker must learn what works by trusting one's body-wisdom, and ultimately, this understanding comes from experience in collaboration with trusted helpers (human and other than human in the physical and non-physical worlds).

Our ancestors knew how to listen, and we have this ability in us, too. For seekers who do not have access to an established Animist heritage, this solitary learning path can be thought of as a journey without any tangible maps. There is guidance available, yet you must feel your way down the path. It is essential to remember that your DNA has memory and you can nudge it awake. The stories and exercises that follow are offered to help you do just that.

A JOURNAL AS ALLY

Writing in a journal can be a part of your spiritual experience. If you are seeking a deeper connection with your inner self, apart from what people tell you to think and feel, you need a confidant that does not speak. You need to speak. Speak your feelings to your journal (digital or paper). When you write and date your first entry, you mark the beginning of a new healing cycle.

*Now we add "Written Exercises"
to our Unfolding Process…*

WRITTEN EXERCISE:

Find a notebook, or make a file on your favorite device, to become your journal for the process of weaving your way through this book. Take a few moments to write your first entry. What would you like to say? Maybe you can start by describing your feelings about the material presented so far, or an event that happened recently. Let your mind wander and you will begin writing. There is no way to fail.

May the boulders of life hold space
for your growing branches.

THE QUESTION IS…"AM I CRAZY"?

When we attempt to connect more deeply with our inner world, many of us secretly fear that the voices inside us are bad or crazy. Voices of inner colonizers tell us that if we hear the voices of the living world, including the world inside our head, we enter into the abyss of craziness. I believe this is why many resist going within. Most wrestle with "Am I crazy because strange things happen in my mind?" & "If I open to the world of what people call spirits, will I become crazy?", which is completely understandable.

It is good to acknowledge that many Animist ways were, and still are, considered evil, weird or crazy in the dominant culture, and you may have voices in your head that tell you so. However, the truth is that communicating with animals and helpers in the physical and non-physical worlds, embracing and creating trance through rhythm, conducting ritual and communicating with the Web of Life are beautiful and needed Animist ways. It is an important time to recognize the moments when you are reluctant to accept these practices out of a deep handed down fear, which might sound something like, "If someone who has power over me thinks I'm crazy for any reason, they can hurt me, slander me, steal from me, fire me, drug, imprison or kill me." One is not wrong to think this way, but do not give in to it.

We live in a culture that has a long history of people's lives being ruined and killed for practicing the Animist arts, sometimes merely speaking of them. Each person drawn to Animism has multiple ancestors who were killed, tortured and/or property and land taken by speaking of, and communicating with, Earth's voices and the voices within. It is now well documented that people who live through trauma are affected in ways that alter their personalities and life survival techniques. This is commonly known today as Post Traumatic Stress. These changes are passed on through generational beliefs, speech and behaviors and are often referred to as Multigenerational Trauma.

When people are persecuted and colonized over many generations, precious knowledge is either "forgotten" or buried deep underground for safekeeping. Traumas from colonization, monotheism and patriarchy created a sickness that deeply infected European ancestors, who then spread the same traumatizing practices around the world. We are all uniquely ready to address these traumas in Self, Family, Community and Culture so we can remember how to flourish together.

WRITTEN EXERCISES:
1. *Have you been told you are crazy? When and by whom?*
2. *Have you felt crazy because of things that happen in your head? Describe how this occurs.*
3. *What have others told you about having voices in the head?*
4. *What attitudes did you grow up with regarding those who just "know" things?*

INNER VOICES
We all hear voices in our heads, whether we call them thoughts, our inner critic, our higher self, spirits, angels or demons.
For our colonized ancestors, it was not beneficial to admit that one heard voices or spirits because this was considered crazy, or worse, of the devil. There is much trauma to heal around this natural part of being human in a living world. In this chapter, the word "voices" is used for what many Animist cultures may call "spirits." Non-physical Spirits have voices, other physical beings besides humans have voices, we each have multiple aspects of our personality that have voices, and they all are perceived by us.
This is not crazy. It is time to learn more about voices you hear and to whom they belong.

When you consider these thoughts/voices/spirits, do not give any of them the power of being "you", "right" or "true." Understand that many voices have been recorded in your mind from those around you, trauma you have experienced, and the culture in which you live. They are not yours just because they are in your head. The purpose of these stories and exercises is to find the origin of each voice. As you assess each origin, you have the power to decide which thoughts or attitudes you believe to be true about yourself. If you are interested in healing and strengthening your Animist nature, it is essential that you have the courage to look at the spirit voices that haunt you and hold you back. Make friends with them, get them to help you or send them on their way. In order to do this, first learn who they are.

Once you learn to discern the bully voices in your head from the other helpful voices, then you can practice communicating with those within you who are looking out for your best interests. Whether you call them helpers, ancestors, guides, powers or spirits, the most important thing is to learn to strengthen your ability to communicate with them. This is done with practice and with guidance from more experienced practitioners in the physical and non-physical worlds. The exercises and stories that follow are offered to help you in this process.

ACTIVITY:
-Any time you are living your life and a voice comes into your head (it may feel like a thought) that says something mean, angry, critical, happy, nervous, doubtful or sad to you, stop and take note. Do your best to simply notice it, note your first reaction, and then write about it. What did the voice say? What emotion did you feel as it spoke to you? Was it a voice that you recognize from your life? What is your first response each time it happens?
-For 1 day, and then 3 days, and then maybe 7 days, track the voices that speak in your mind and write about them. The more you know about the voices that reside inside you, the less power they have over you. The destination, if there is one, is to be in cooperation more often with the voices you hear within, and to cast out or transform the voices that are not helpful.

BEFRIENDING DETHRONING VOICES
Colonized people have been taught that hearing voices is something to avoid. Due to this belief, we hide the reality of hearing voices, even the helpful ones. Once you begin to listen within without fear, there are many voices that can help you learn how to tend your trauma and

remember how to use your abilities for the good of your Kindred. Trust that you have benevolent mentors and allies within and around you and they are looking out for you.

The way to understand the messages from helpful voices is to first learn to tame the discounting voices within. By the time we are adults, our brains have absorbed many self-negating voices from the dominant culture every day through school, media and family. These voices have become so engrained in our minds that after a while they become permanent residents, speaking up at the most inopportune moments with one cruel thought or another. "You're stupid," "You can't do that," "You're not pretty enough for that," "Who do you think you are, anyway? Needless to say, these voices are *not* helpful.

Please note: When I speak of listening to the voices that speak to you, I am *not* referring to any voices that tell you to do harmful things to yourself or others. If you have voices in your head that command you to do things that you do not want to do, this is called a command hallucination. Please treat this voice with care and speak to someone you trust about it. The most important thing is that you do not give in to the voice and do what it tells you. You are not bad for having one of these voices speak to you, but you may need help in dealing with it. Please talk with a qualified mental health practitioner. *Animism and its forms of practice are not a substitute for mental or physical healthcare.*

WHO ARE ALL THESE VOICES?
I call mine my "orchestra." I have also heard them called a "consensus" and even a "cacophony". Whatever you choose to call them, the important thing is that you admit to yourself that they are there. One voice might belong to your mother or your 4th grade teacher. Hopefully you have some that are friendly and guiding. I have one that feels like a caring fatherly individual. It is not a specific voice from my life, more like an invisible helper that speaks up when I need comfort.

Then there are other voices. Voices that want to put you down or belittle you. Some are purposefully mean and others don't know any better. I do not say this to condone what is said in your head. On the contrary, any voice, thought, or attitude that is not for your highest good must transform itself into one who is supportive of you, or it must be made quiet or to go away. It is important to realize, however, to not go about this process with a hateful attitude. Your goal is to figure out who is saying what in your mind, and then choose who can stay as they are and who needs to change…and to those that will not be helpful, they are not welcome. Your inner world is your sacred space, so protect it. Who do you hear in your head?

May the blessings of your Allies
be felt by you always.

CONNECTING: ANCESTORS & ALLIES

"I traveled to a forest and enjoyed rolling in the dark earth as wolf. Then I tumbled down a tunnel and at the end was a door that looked like a round cap. I opened it and stepped into a deep forest and many animals were there: Deer, Bear, Butterfly and many others. I had the feeling that this was their home. They were very social with each other. It was a party. When I stepped through the door, one of them saw me and exclaimed, "She's here!" Everyone was excited to see me. I felt touched because I realized that I had made it to their world. In a previous journey I had asked about my guides, and I was brought here. I asked the partygoers, "Are any of you my guides?" They laughed and lovingly said not to ask such stupid questions." (one of Quynn's first inner world journeys-1996)

My understanding of Animist cultures includes the reality that we each have a gathering of helpful physical and non-physical allies and ancestors who can help us. However, the dominant culture is uncomfortable with the idea of speaking to those that we cannot physically see, so we tend to hide the connections with non-physical allies, or alliances with ones who are perceived as "things" such as Trees, Water, Air, Stones etc. Many ancestors have been ridiculed, imprisoned or murdered for speaking of these alliances. The existence of a non-physical reality plays a central role in Animist life and is generally considered "normal". Communicating with the non-physical energies that are here with us has always been understood to be a natural part of being Human.

Asking for help from benevolent allies within and around us is an experience that all humans share, whether people call it prayer, dreaming, journeying or divination. Since the beginning of time, when humans need to make a decision, want to heal, need an easy hunt and abundant food…whatever the reason, when we ask for help from the other realms, it is because we need assistance that we hope is available to us in the moment we need it most. Communication (whether human, other than human, or spirit (beyond the physical world) consists of talking *and* listening. You are invited to practice connecting through the two exercises shared below.

SPIRIT WORLD CONNECTION RITUAL:
-When you are ready, find a private space that feels safe and quiet. It could be inside or outside. Create a circle around the space any way that you want to. You could mark it with rocks, string or even stars in your mind. As you do this, focus your attention on your safety and wellbeing, and say your own version of the following to yourself, "I welcome helpers, spirits and ancestors that are for my highest good. I am protected. I trust my intuition. I am guided."

-Place a cloth or bandana over your eyes (this helps with self-consciousness and keeps the outside world at bay). Focus your attention on your center, wherever you perceive it to be, and breathe into that place.

-When you feel ready, begin talking (out loud or in your mind) to your spirit helpers. Speak as if they are actually listening. If you don't know who to talk to, express that. Express your feelings. You can say something like, "I feel stupid talking to someone that I can't see, but here I am." Say whatever comes to your mind. Do this until you begin to relax, and then do it a bit more.

-If you are curious, focus on your ancestors. Say hello to them (whether you know them or not). Ask a question. Share from your heart, even about challenges you feel. You are attempting to bridge a gap that has kept you and your helpful ancestral spirits apart for too long. Perfection is not expected.

-If you are not sure what to say, sit with an open heart. What do you feel? Do not dismiss any feelings. If you hear any judging or doubting voices in your head ("this is stupid," or "you can't do this"), GREAT! You have just identified a voice in your head that you can deal with later. Note it in your mind and return to the task at hand. You may not be able to "hear" your allies but they can talk to you through feelings and thoughts in your mind. Talk and listen until you feel finished for this moment.

-When you feel ready, offer gratitude for the connection. You might also thank your self for being willing to open yourself to this communication. Do this in a way that feels right to you. Imagine that you close the circle for now.

-After the circle is closed, remain open to your spirit world guidance. Write about what happened, or what didn't seem to happen. Take note of any unhelpful or negating voices or feelings that emerged. Write them down to "call them out" when you are ready, as ones who need to transform, or ultimately leave your space.

May the tidal Ocean beings teach you
about your waves of emotion.

INNER COUNCIL MEDITATION

This exercise is for you to meet some of your inner guides. You could listen to a drumbeat, rattle, meditation music, or in silence.

-Put yourself in a comfortable position, close your eyes and breathe. After a few breaths, imagine yourself in a place in Nature, the first place that comes to your mind. In your inner vision, take note of where you are. You may see this place as if watching a movie, or you could also have a thought or feeling of a place. All ways are valid. Take a moment and notice how you feel about this imaginary place. When you feel comfortable, look for a place near you that catches your attention and go there in your mind. When you get there ask to meet members of your "inner council" (those helpers who are with you consistently).

-Imagine that a circle appears before your eyes. You begin to get a feeling, vision or thought about who is around the circle. Just stare at the circle with your inner eyes and allow your mind to show you who is there through impression or imagination. Ask for an image, thought, or feeling to come to you. Helpers can take any form. Animals, Humans, Hybrids, Plants, Lights, Colors, Energies with no form… All are valid.

-You may feel or see a helper in the circle, or you may get a flash/thought of a helper in your mind. Remember to be kind with yourself. If your imaging or concentration skills seem weak or distracted, don't get frustrated; just relax, and keep your focus on calming your body with breath.

-If you feel the information you are receiving does not meet your expectations, change your tactics. Try asking in your mind to meet one of your helpers, and then relax and listen with your body. If any thought, image or feeling comes to you about an animal or guide, take note. Something is being revealed to you.

-If, at any time, you receive information and you want to know more, relax and ask a question in your mind. You do not need to speak with your mouth to speak in the spirit world. All you need is to ask in your mind and they can hear you. As an example, let's say you are greeted by an animal.

You could ask the animal any of the following questions:
"What wisdom do you have for me?"
"Is there anything you need to tell me?"
"What can I do for you?"

-After you ask, then listen with your entire body. Do not discount what comes to you. You may not see how what came to you may relate to you, but do not doubt. Remember to welcome any information that comes to you.

-There are many ways one can practice this exercise. You can imagine the circle and see who shows up, then attempt to speak with each one (if more than one shows themself). Or, you can see them one at a time. You might only connect with one helper. The spirit world gives us what we need most at the moment. If you connect with one, focus on that one and offer gratitude. Trust that more will reveal themselves when it is time.

-If you do not receive clear communication from any particular guide, do not fret. Instead, ask, "Why did no one come?" Notice your feelings, as well as any impressions that may come to you. Also, if one presents itself, but not clearly, take a moment and focus more intently on the subject. Instead of looking for it, try feeling it. Sometimes we need to be creative to let these helpers show themselves in their own way. The most important thing is to not feel rejected or to say, "See, it doesn't work!" Think of this process as making a friend. You may need to try more than once to connect clearly.

You may face certain attitudes from your mind or your culture about this process. You may hear an inner voice that says, "This isn't real," "This is ridiculous," or "You can't do this". If this happens to you, take note of the voice(s) but do not give in to them. Just keep practicing and trying to connect in different ways. The point of listening within is to strengthen your relationship with your intuition and to strengthen your center. You have a lot of help available to you when you know you can ask for it.

WRITTEN EXERCISE:
Write about your experience with the above exercises. Let yourself write as much as you need to describe the experiences adequately.

May your altars be clear and vibrant!

THE SPIRIT BRIDGE PRACTITIONER

Throughout the story of humanity, our ancestors lived and flourished in communities on every landmass of the Earth. Healers of mind, body and spirit were needed in every community. In the Kindred of Web of Life Animists, these healers are called Spirit Bridge Practitioners. This means they are "called" by their ancestors to be a bridge to the spirit world for their community. The calling to this life could come in two different ways. The first way is if a person is born or adopted into a family of Animist Practitioners, they might be expected to follow the Animist healer's path. This was called "Inherited Ability." The other way is when a person experiences a "spontaneous calling," such as a near death experience, healing from a profound sickness or some other extraordinary event. This last experience is what happened for me, and there are many others who have been called in a similar way today, and in the past. It has always been this way.

There are signs when Spirit Bridge abilities emerge within a person. Some examples include: visions, dreams, hearing voices, the ability to go places in the mind, sensing the other beings in Nature, "knowing" things, premonitions, experiencing a strange sickness from which they heal, and synchronistic encounters with nature beings. Each calling experience is unique. It is hard to know how *you* will end up working with your abilities until you dive in to training.

Resources for training: https://weboflifeanimists.com/online-learning/

A Spirit Bridge practitioner's art is to be a tender of the soul and its' healing. Many people are artistic, and everyone has a creative spirit, but for someone to become an "artist," one lives as an artist. This includes dedication to the path, sacrifice for the cause of learning, deep patience and practice, practice, practice. When one is called to the art of healing practitionership, it is helpful to listen and act upon it.

WRITTEN EXERCISES
-Write about a "psychic" or "intuitive" experience, a dream that guided you or a synchronicity that could not be denied.
-Has there been anyone in your family tree who was known to "know" things, have healing abilities or prophetic dreams?
-What is/was the attitude of those around you about these occurrences?
-Do/did you follow a religion (such as Christianity, Islam, Judaism, etc.) and how does that religion view the aspects of Animism (such as prophetic dreams, psychic or intuitive knowing, and/or Personhood for Other than Human Kin).

I end this chapter with a message from a guiding dream. It was a message for me, and now it is for you.

"Go! Expand into who you are.
Your ancestors have been killed in the past for being who they were.
You are needed now, so go forth!
We (the collective consciousness/ancestors)
support you in your endeavor."

To dive deeper, explore the Introduction to Intuitive Animism course:
weboflifeanimists.com/product/beginning-the-journey-intro-to-intuitive-animism/

Coupon code available in end pages

May your inner flowers be pollinated
for creativity to come.

Chapter Two
CONNECTING WITHIN

The power to imagine
shows you how to find
that you can go anywhere
with your sacred mind.
This thing we call Imagination
has been on the decline
because we hear what happens there
is "only in our mind."
Yet our allies come to guide us
They take us near and far
to all the dreamlike places
where our kindred are.
Go there, come back,
listen to what they say.
Bring back healing love notes
that show us Nature's ways
of health, peace and balance
in ourselves and within our kind.
When we remember ourselves
our sacred world speaks
and all life on this planet thrives.

WELCOME TO YOUR HOME WITHIN
It is important to remember that you have a benevolent and sacred inner world that is worth protecting, and having one is a natural part of being a Human Being.

The realms inside each of us, as the dominant culture instructs us to experience it, is only a fraction of the possibilities of what we call Reality. There are many aspects of the multidimensional worlds within us that the colonized culture does not consider real, and anyone who feels, sees and experiences other layers of reality can be considered crazy. Everyone has an inner landscape and every person has their own way(s) of sensing, seeing, feeling, hearing or perceiving these inner realms.

Ways to connect are ultimately infinite, and include daydreaming, imagination, also dreaming, visioning, trance, meditating, channeling, intuition, plant assistance and so many others. If you have any feelings of concern or fear about having an "inner world", or if you doubt that you have one, then this is a perfect time to address this colonized inner voice, and ask your allies and ancestors for healing and teachings that can help you feel more comfortable.

While you may not connect within in the same ways as are described in this chapter, the intent of these words and ideas is to inspire you to explore ways to connect with the inner realms, including characters, ancestors and allies that you knew as a child and maybe before you were born. As you have grown into adulthood, you have likely been informed that this connection is not real or not open to you anymore.

To reacquaint yourself with your inner wilderness, even if your relationship has grown distant or estranged, is a powerful act of reclamation and self-care (see chapter 7 Rhythms of Feather and Smoke for more self-care ideas). As an adult you may have had to make yourself "hard" or "closed" in certain places to succeed and even simply stay alive. You may have had to "forget" certain things to be content with adult life and to survive in this culture. Trust that your inner world has much to share with you and know that your inner world is woven together with the world around you in a synchronistic, even a magical, way.

WRITTEN EXERCISE:
-Do you remember a connection (through imagination, make-believe or daydreaming) with an inner world as a child?
-What was your most recent dream, message, synchronicity?
-Have you had an experience that was different than how you were taught about "Reality"? Write about it.

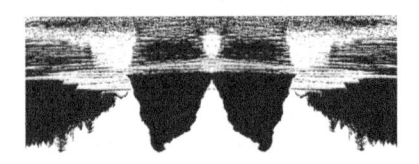

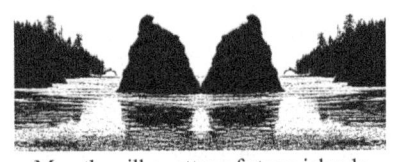

May the silhouettes of stone islands
speak kindly to you.

A NOTE-
If you are new to meditation, or what simply might be called "Calm Mind", the words below are for you.
For those who have an active relationship with your calm mind, you are welcome to skim the words below and jump to "Imagination".

BEGINNER'S MIND to CALM MIND
To expand your ability to connect with your inner world, it is helpful to expand your practice of calming your mind. Focusing on gentle sounds, breathing consciously, and having calming experiences in Nature are great ways to quiet the chatter. The goal is to be able to help the inner monkeys to settle down, to become more like a still pond than a speedy river. The still pond becomes a mirror, reflecting whatever is nearby. Learning to quiet the mind allows you to learn what thoughts, feelings, memories are inside you, as well as what inhibits you from feeling centered. This is the side of meditation that people often don't understand, or don't like. Calming the mind can invite discordant

feelings, challenging feelings or unhelpful thoughts to come to the surface so you can realize they are there. Don't be afraid of this step, it is a necessary part of the inner exploration process.

A peaceful mind is not a destination, "achieving" it once and forever. It is a constant dance between you and the voices in your head, your thoughts and emotions. As we age and grow, our ways of quiet mind change as well, so if something that used to "work" doesn't now, take it as a sign of growth and explore new ways to feel centered within yourself. Some days it will take everything you have to get an unhelpful voice in your mind to shut up. Hopefully there will be many other times when you are calm without even trying. The most important thing is to hold the intention to be as calm as possible, in every moment, and then to practice in some way every day.

Some "Calm Mind" practices focus on being able to rid the mind of *all* thought. As a beginner, I found that to be irritating because the moment the thoughts subsided, my mind said, "Hey, no thought!" and that in itself, was a thought. The point is not to fight the thoughts, but rather to allow thoughts to move through your mind without grabbing hold of them. Over time, this practice allows inner calm to exist without the chattering mind being able to take over. A calm mind also creates a jumping off point for the inner journeying process (later in this chapter).

Calm where you are:
You can calm your mind anywhere in this busy world, and it is helpful to teach yourself to do this, but it is also important for you to be able to retreat from the loudness of life when needed. Depending on your ability to have privacy at home, your special space could be a room that feels good to you, where you can shut the door to roommates or family. It could be a place in Nature or in the human world (even your car!), but pick a place where you can quiet yourself and listen within without being startled. If you do not feel you have a safe place to do this, then my humble opinion is to first focus on finding a quiet nook, corner, pillow or car seat for this work. As you create space for your sacred self, your mind will be more calm during your practices.

"The way past blockages is to move through them. This takes courage, dedication and patience. I know that it can be done" (1999).

May the Waterfall help your heart overflow with nourishment.

THE POWER OF IMAGINATION
The degree to which you move forward on your path of inner world exploration is directly related to the relationship you have with your imagination.

As children, we had an inherent sense of imagination, but for most, at a certain age, we were encouraged to turn our backs on it. Many realize the need to search for it later in life, people like you and me.

Take a moment and stop reading to look around your physical space. Notice things that are useful to you or that mean something to you. Whatever you choose to look at comes from someone's imagination, maybe yours. Art, furniture, cars, technology, music, video games and everything else around you emerged from our individual and collective imagination. While the beauty and interconnectedness of Nature was not created by the human mind, it was imagined by something, and created somehow, and it is fantastic…isn't it?!

It is the unshackling of our collective imagination that has brought our technology to the point where it is now. Our collective imaginations will take us into our future. If we have a healthy, free, and active imagination, we can create a better world. "We" includes you.

There are many ideas about imagination in the dominant culture, both positive and negative. Saying someone has "an active imagination" can be meant as a compliment, dismissal or judgment. First, you must realize that you do have an imagination, and when well fed and trained, it is one of your most precious tools for feeling centered. By "trained," I do not mean "controlled."
I mean for the two of you to learn to become a team. You and your imagination are a strong, creative pair.

QUESTIONS TO PONDER:
-What thoughts, memories or feelings come to you when you think of imagination?
-How was your imagination valued by your childhood culture?
-When did you put away any favorite "imaginary" ideas associated with childhood?

WRITTEN EXERCISE:
Write your feelings about imagination in general, and then about your connection with your imagination in this moment.

INNER IMAGININGS
Imagination speaks in many ways, including images, emotions, and thoughts. When practicing the art of listening to one's imagination, there is no one thing that you are listening for. When you are open to what is already there revealing itself, it always does in one way or another.

Many modern colonized people have a strong inner dialog that is not calm. If, when you listen within, you hear your own voice doubting you or taunting you, congratulations. You have just connected with something that is causing you stress, and stress affects the body and the mind in unhelpful ways. You can use the Spirit World Journey (which comes later in this chapter) and journaling to dialog with this voice within you. If you have a calm inner feeling that leaves you feeling centered, congratulations, you are at peace at that moment. Remember this moment the next time you feel stressed.

The point of the following exercise is to hear/sensing what your inner world, and in this case your body, may be telling you about things in your life that are stressful.

EXERCISE:
-Close your eyes and your body breathe. Place your attention on any area of discomfort (tension, tightness, pain) and listen again. How does it feel? What thoughts, images and feelings come to you when you notice this place in your body?
-Listen to it. What is it communicating? Is it a thought in your own voice, or is it someone else's? How do you feel when the thought is there?
-When you listen to your body, do you feel sadness, anger, irritation or worry? Where is it? Can you breathe into it?
Hone in on the place where the emotion takes you. Listen again. Do any thoughts come to your mind when you have your attention and breath on the feeling?

Sadness and Tears: If you feel sadness when doing this, or any other inner connection exercise, let it be, even if the feeling brings tears. If your body wants to cry, assume that it needs to release. Trust your body and accept the sadness. Do you notice any thoughts or memories seemingly related to the tears? Even if the memories or thoughts do not seem related, take note of them anyway. They are potentially linked with the well of emotion within you. Please understand that with attention, sadness and other challenging emotions do not have to be bottomless and endless. If it seems endless or overwhelming, *please reach out to a healing helper or support group online or in person.*

If you feel some form of static or distraction within you when you attempt the above exercises, be with it. In this chapter and beyond, you will learn ways to do this effectively. The power of imagination is the ability to imagine something different than what is. Decide that your imagination is a helpful friend. In a tight spot, you need to be able to creatively think yourself out of the situation. The same is true in your inner world. We are all dealing with many "tight spots" as we live in the world around us. We all want our minds to be as unburdened and fully functional as possible. Often, your inner world speaks in symbols, codes and patterns. This wisdom can best be understood with your imaginative mind, with what I call the Spirit World Journey.

"Last night I got in touch with a beautiful turquoise iridescent serpent with peacock-like feathers. He (he felt like a he) appeared to me and we began flying. We flew up through the clouds and then we dissipated into atoms. I was instantly aware of the Earth's breath and heartbeat. It was synonymous with mine." (1996).

May the sacred spiral of Pine cones
bring you clues to guide your journeys.

SPIRIT WORLD JOURNEYS

"Spirit World Journey" refers to the act of tuning in to your spirit world/dreaming mind while listening to consistent rhythmic sound including drum or rattle. This simple, yet profound act allows people access to the realms that are generally thought to be available to all little children, in our dream time, with plant teachers, and as we prepare to pass from this life.

The act of focusing inward with intention can bring helpful messages, sensations and connections with non-physical teachers, ancestors and guardians that have been with you since before you were born. We all have an internal guidance system that may take any form, such as animals, colors, ancestors, angels, or no form at all. Trust that these non-physical allies want to help you in ways that are most needed, and they can activate your authentic self in this life and beyond.

This ancient trance practice has always been with humans, and it is available to YOU, right now. While I call this process a Spirit World Journey, you may have heard it called a "Shamanic" Journey.

This general practice can help you tune into your own wisdom and remind you that you are not alone in this world. Soul wounds, from this life and before, can be helpfully approached with this practice. Listening to or making rhythm with a drum or a rattle, plus focused intention and sustained attention is an enlightening act that can guide you when you need it.

THE RHYTHM WITHIN
While meditations without any sound accompaniment can be very helpful, many people use rhythm to help them take their inner journey. I began journeying without listening to rhythm because I had not thought to do so. Soon after, a young Indigenous healer told me to look for a piece of music that spoke to me, something rhythmic and repetitive (such as drums, didgeridoo, or rattle) because the sounds would help me journey. She said it would help "keep me there." In fact, almost every culture with Animist roots explores the realms of reality with the aid of some form of rhythm to enter trance. Repetitive sound quickly lowers our brain waves into a state more closely to where they are when we dream at night. One way to describe the process is to say that consistent rhythms open your dreaming mind while your discerning mind is awake, thereby enhancing your ability to be in "both worlds". You can listen to any piece of music that is rhythmic, monotonous, and most importantly, that you feel the rhythm calling to you. If you feel called to drum or rattle for yourself, it adds a whole other layer of trance. This can be more challenging for beginners, but the way to improve is to PRACTICE.

HOW DO I?...
Our Spirit Worlds speak to us through the languages of signs, symbols, messages and synchronicity. Many people in modern culture have forgotten the intricacy of these languages. As you learn to understand your intuition and how the Universe speaks to you, you will more accurately understand this wisdom as it guides you through your life. Here are some things to keep in mind that might help:

The main ingredients in being able to journey within for guidance:
-What is your intention for this journey? What do you need? Write out a question to clearly state your intention. Carry that question/issue into the drumming.

-Know that you have protectors who are looking out for you.
-It is your right and responsibility to call upon them for assistance.
-Trust that what comes to you is for your best interest, and if you desire, at any time you can tell it to "go away".
-You belong in your Inner World and it is always with you.

While listening to the rhythm, if you are unsure about any of these ingredients, ask within for help in that moment. If you are still not convinced, open your eyes. When you feel safe, begin again to listen to the rhythm and restate your intention.

During the rhythm, allow the images, feelings, impressions and thoughts to appear and let them lead you. A message can come to you as a vision, thought, feeling, sound or memory. The information that follows may feel surreal, unexpected or illogical to your mind. Trust yourself and your growing connections and ask for more clarity.

Keep in mind that the spirit world journey is an interactive experience. If you find yourself stuck or in the dark, don't panic. You can be creative about how to change the situation because it is *your* dreamlike inner world. Anything you can do in a dream, you can do in a journey. A telepathic conversation can unfold into detailed, meaningful and much needed answers to questions you may not have known exactly how to articulate. Simple questions such as "Why can't I see?" or "What do I need to do to move on?" or "Who here has a message for me?" can bring important connections.

Another bit of advice: If an animal, voice or image first presents itself and you don't like it for some reason, don't try to change it to something else. Let the original animal stay. Trust that it came for a reason. Every helper has wisdom, even if it isn't what you expected.

May the portals to the lower world
benevolently show themselves to you.

Tips for Enhancing your Tuning In Journeys:

-Receive a free 6 minute drum track w/ coupon code "wisdom" here: weboflifeanimists.com/product-category/free-offerings/

-To begin, listen to your rhythmic music.

-Relax, close your eyes, ponder your question, and ask for help.

-You are not going anywhere that is foreign or dangerous. This is your inner world.

-Always follow what first comes to your mind. If you ask for an animal helper and an ant appears, don't try to change it to something different. Ask ant for its wisdom.

-If you get stuck, or are unsure, ask a question. At any time, ask for help and be open to receive guidance.

-If you begin to feel that you are thinking or forcing your way through the journey (instead of letting it come to you), pause, breathe and listen to the music/drum.

-If you experience something that seems painful, breathe and ask a question ("Why am I experiencing this?" or, "Who can help me?").

-If you need clarity, assistance or a travel guide, ask.

-The best way to learn about the spirit world journeying process is to allow it to teach you when you practice doing it.

-If you have thoughts that feel like distractions, focus on those thoughts after the journey. What thoughts came to your mind during the rhythm? How are they important to you?

Technical Assistance for Strengthening your Practice:
-Find a quiet and private space.
-Allow your body to settle in a comfortable position. If your body needs to change positions or begin to move, follow your inclinations.
-If you cannot be in a dark space, you can put something over your eyes so that your inner palette is more colorful.
-Headphones/Earbuds allow surround sound.
-Write down your experiences, including your doubts and questions.

ANCESTORS AND ALLIES

A vital part of Animism is the understanding that each of us has ancestors and allies that look out for us. Animist cultures describe these non-physical relationships in different ways, and why they may present themselves for a variety of reasons. If you do not have a direct connection to your Animist ancestry, you can still learn about your own guidance system. You do this by connecting with your spirit world again and again, and asking for them to make themselves known to you. Your most trusted allies are those who show up for you over time and they can be quite creative in the ways they help you in both the spirit and the physical world.

May your roots help you pass
through the eye to the treefull sky.

GOING IN AND THROUGH

When I first began to quiet my mind (while counting my breaths), and even before I knew what a Spirit World Journey was, I saw a tunnel in

my mind's eye and I felt that I was plummeting down it. After this happened multiple times, someone gave me Michael Harner's book, *The Way of the Shaman*. I was surprised to read about a tunnel in this book, and when I did, I knew that what was happening to me has happened to others. Traditional Shamans travel this tunnel to get to the Spirit World.
I was relieved and humbled that the tunnel was shared with me.

Since the beginning of my Animist life as described above, I have journeyed many, many times and sat with many people in journey circles. I have come to believe that there are many ways to travel to the spirit world, not all journey with or through a tunnel. It is good to know, however, that if you feel a tumbling, spinning or falling feeling, you are likely feeling the sensations of the tunnel or portal between worlds. If you can allow yourself to stop resisting or fearing it, it can then bring you to an important place for needed information.

THREE WORLDS
Many cultures feel that there are three worlds, the upper, middle and lower worlds. However, unlike in Christianity, in spirit world journeying, there is no judgment about the meaning of these worlds, as in one being bad and one being good. There are different reasons and ways that a journeyer can travel down into the Earth and reach the lower world, or travel up beyond the sky to connect with the upper world. The middle world is where we live, and during a journey you can travel in time and space in this world. You can travel to the lower world in many ways, including going through an animal hole, water, tree roots, or a flower stem. You can travel to the upper world through a tree, a rainbow or with a bird. In any of these "places," you can fly, change your size and breathe under water. Your spirit world will show you how, if, and when, you are meant to go down, or up in this way.

YOUR INNER SENSES
While in the dream-like mindset of journeying, all your senses are available to you. You may hear, see, feel, sense, smell and taste things while in a journey. Sometimes your senses might even feel super-powered. When needed, your senses can, and will, alert you to needed

information and opportunities for healing. Journeying is a powerful and gentle practice to help you learn to trust them.

SACRED DRUMBEATS
Turning within, while listening to a drum, has no boundaries.

The sounds of drumbeats have been with humans since we became human. It doesn't take work to be affected by the repetitive rhythms because the drumbeat is in us, in our hearts and pumping blood.

When you are ready to join the drumbeats for a journey, prepare your space so you are comfortable. Settle into your body and offer gratitude for something, anything. Then focus on your breath. When you feel centered, ask for assistance, imagine or choose a starting place in nature, and then state your intention. At any point in the process, you are encouraged to ask for an ally. Trust that you are supported.

In your inner world you have abilities like in a dream. You can fly, think yourself to a new place and many other fantastical possibilities. After you state your intention and ask for help, look for an entry and go towards any opening that calls to you. In the past I have entered the spirit world through a flower stem, by diving into water and by shooting up a tree. I have also felt a "place" emerge around me, a scene or a feeling…and I just go with it. You can, too. Remember that your inner world is revealing itself to you and trying to teach you. You have help, you will meet guides and you may come up against obstacles. You may see, hear, sense, feel, remember, or think things. Your goal is to absorb information and to learn the ropes, so to speak, of how to travel through your inner world for needed guidance.

If you experience difficulties, do not assume that you are unable to journey, explore the difficulty instead. If you feel scattered, maybe your life is so hectic that it is a challenge to relax and concentrate. If so, listen to the drum and breathe or rest until you feel more relaxed. There is no pressure to have to see anything. If you feel scared or tired, try asking within about the issue that makes you feel scared or tired. You are navigating through a seemingly new world and there will be many new things to learn and understand, yet you have the instruction book in your cells. Trust this to be true.

When the rhythm stops, it indicates the end of this particular journey, for the moment. Offer gratitude and find your way back to the place in Nature where you started. You can go back the same way that you came, or creatively think yourself back another way. To "come back" means to bring your spirit body back into your physical body and when you feel completely present, open your eyes.

WHAT DO YOU NEED?
You are encouraged to practice by listening to drum or rattle while pondering the following intentions for your journeys, or ask about something that is real for you right now:
-Ask for a guide who is ready to help you
-Journey to your Center (of your body/soul)
-Connect with an ally for what you need now (what do you need now?)
-You could imagine the land of your dreams to ask for a dream mentor for guidance about something that is important to you.
-In any scenario, you could ask, "What wisdom do you have for me?" or "What do I need to know to feel peace and balance in my life?" or a question that comes to you.

WRITTEN EXERCISE:
Write about your journeys, meditations, or insights. Note any difficulties and any guides that you encountered. How did you feel during each journey?

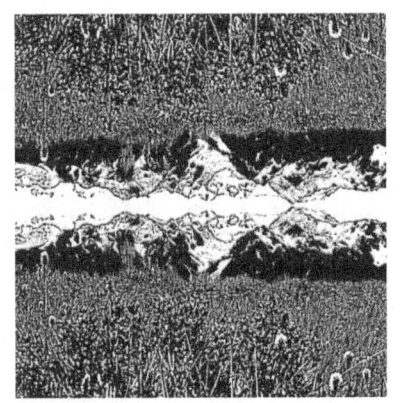

May the high mountain peaks within you nourish
your inner flower meadows.

EMOTIONAL JOURNEYS

While journeys can be relaxing, nourishing, surreal and dreamlike, sometimes going within can unearth emotional unrest or discomfort from past experiences. If this happens, please resist the impulse to push the feelings away or think that something is wrong with you. The purpose of connecting with your inner world is to learn more about yourself and the nature of reality, connect with guidance larger than you, and tend trauma that is yet untended. This means that if there is something hiding inside that wants to "get out" and be seen or heard, it can make itself known in this process. If, and when, you experience something that is uncomfortable or troubling call on a guide, helper or ancestor to come and be with you during your journey. Below is an example from a past circle:

Once, a young woman journeyed for the first time. She was nervous, but ready to try it. Her story after the journey was amazing, so I'll share it with you.

She said that she found herself in the house in which she grew up. I got the feeling by the way that she spoke of the house that something bad happened to her there. In her journey she was in her bedroom as a girl. She was in bed, and she immediately felt fear because as a girl she had many nightmares of a monster that came out of the closet and killed her. In this journey, as she watched the closet, the monster indeed came out of the closet to get her. Instead of succumbing to this beast, in this journey she asked for help and immediately grew to a large size and her body began to pulsate with energy. She went to the monster and, as she put it, "kicked its ass." It felt so good for her to do this that she then went back and did it again and the monster went away. When she told the group this story she was beaming. In this journey, her inner world animated in a way to help her get rid of a past "monster" that in some way was ruling her life.

If a monster presents itself in a journey, be creative about how you want to deal with it. Ask for help! You have more help available to you than you know. Remember, this is YOUR world.

If you feel overwhelmed by anything in your journey and you cannot get around it within a journey, reach out to someone in the physical world that you trust for assistance. You are invited to look through www.weboflifeanimists.com for free offerings, writings or services, including live online "Journey Circles" I offer each month. (https://weboflifeanimists.com/events/)

When you have a question or you feel you want a "dreaming mind" perspective about your life, you can use this practice to see what comes to you. You can ask, "What do I need to know about this issue," or you can ask for an animal helper to give you advice. Know that you have a pantheon of helpers to assist you in maneuvering through life with grace and flow. They have been with you since your beginning, and it is time to call upon them again.

WRITTEN EXERCISE:
Think of issues that are important to you in your life right now. Create a list of journey intentions that might be helpful to you. Use this list as your next set of journeys.

EXCERPTS FROM MY JOURNEYS
I have included some excerpts from my own early journeying journals to show a variety of possibilities. I hope these journeying examples are helpful to you as you explore your own inner worlds.

CALM WATER JOURNEY
I was very confused about two things in my life. A couple of days later I had a journey—I was in the middle of water, a pond. There was a dense fog. I could only see about ten feet around me. I was calm and the water was, too. In one direction, there were reeds in the water. Then I heard someone call my name, softly beckoning me. Then there was another voice calling to me from another place on the pond's banks. I didn't know which way to go. I listened to my heart and still didn't know. Then voices were calling to me from all around the pond. I felt pulled. I couldn't decide which direction to go. Then I realized it wasn't time to decide. The fog was there because I couldn't see the whole picture to know what to do. I then heard an internal voice "relax. enjoy the wait," so I did. I focused on floating (1997).

WINGED GUIDE JOURNEY
I got the feeling of a guide, he is a fairy. He said that he has been showing himself to me by projecting himself as butterfly. He has wings in fairy form. He said I am one of the winged creatures. They (fairies)

bless me with gifts of their feathers and presence. (Today, twice a bird flew over me and cawed.) After a while I remembered to ask if he had any gifts for me. S/he was happy I asked. She put a crystal behind my right eye, for sight, and then a crystal in the sole of my left foot, to feel the rhythm (1997).

BEAR JOURNEY
In another journey, I was on a path and behind me was a bear, a huge brown bear. She pulled me to her and somehow I went inside her. I looked out her eye for a few minutes and then she vomited me back up. As I laid in a fetal position on the ground beneath her, she sliced my face with her paw. She said, "Now you are mine" (1998).

HEARD IN A JOURNEY
"Dear One, I know you feel irritated and stuck and cramped, and you cannot at all foresee the string of events that are coming. Yet each one will deepen you, stretch you, and strengthen you in ways you can only yet imagine. A great change is coming. You know it, you feel it, you want it. The world needs you to stretch and let go of the known, the familiar and the polite. The world is calling you to be dynamic, bold and a bit crazy/sane. You know it is true. Your little death is coming. It is almost here. Here it comes...can you hear its whisper?" (2007)

May the mud pits of Life not burden you today.

ACCESSING TRANCE
Maybe at this point in the chapter you have had amazing meditations, journeys and insights and you can't wait for more! Maybe not so much.

Maybe you don't resonate with the drum, or laying down still, or the idea of journeying. Whatever your experience with the exercises in this chapter, know that activating a sense of trance in your body and mind can happen in many ways, using a variety of methods. It doesn't matter which methods you ultimately use to connect within, what does matter is that you are able to let go and feel the ingredients of trance.

WHAT ARE THE INGREDIENTS?

Slowed breathing, relaxation, a sense of distance from your physical environment, altered time perception, euphoria, a sense of connectedness and sensing impressions, messages, visions, downloads are all potential parts of your trance states. When you experience "trance", let it be. It doesn't need to be "true" or "false". Just engage with it in the moment.

There are many methods of trance state activation that can be helpful. The following list is by no means complete, only a small sample that I have experienced. The goal is to find the ways that work for you.

-Repeated Breathing (deeper and faster, many versions of breathwork are available)
-Repetitive Movement (running, walking, shaking, dancing, spinning, rocking, rattling, drumming, sex)
-Listening to and Creating Rhythm/Sound (singing, humming, drumming, rattling, music, chanting +)
-Plant Medicine (Please use caution about setting, choosing your human guide, timing and feeling called. If you sense doubt or are unsure, wait and journey about it.)

CONTINUING THE JOURNEY

After reading these words, and traveling within during the journeys offered, you may now see the possibilities within the endless nature of your inner wilderness. Each time you set a journey intention, and each ally of the physical and non-physical worlds offers you another perspective to exploring your life and your spiritual path. The beauty of journeying is that each issue is unique, and each journey is different.

During any period of life change you may find that the experiences during various journeys have a similar theme, or maybe they offer exactly the same message again and again. Each time you ask, you have an opportunity to take the advice offered and apply it to your situation. You may also choose to not follow the advice offered. Such is free will. It is your world, and you can do as you want, and what comes of your choice, comes.

What happens if, or when, a journeyer does not want to follow the guidance offered? What if you do not like the message of a journey? This is an interesting opportunity for you to find your truth and learn to understand why your inner guides are saying one thing and you are feeling another. Such a situation can be an excellent reason to journey once more. You could ask why you feel the way you do, or what the message might be. Sometimes an answer simply leads to more questions. If you ever find yourself feeling this way, know that your questions will lead you where you need to be. Trust yourself and your sacred guidance system and know that even when you do not know where you are going, you are being guided. The path is always a winding one.

May the thick bark of your sacred lineage
protect you against unhelpful fires.

I would like to share the following messages of journeyers in past circles, written down immediately after the drum stopped.

"Situations that appear to be tense and chaotic always have a clear, soft pool below that is calm and serene. We can gently find resources within ourselves that create harmony."

"A sea of ants was coming toward me, surrounding me. I knew that feminine energy works well as a group, like ants. Then they began crawling all over me, which felt like a massage. While I tingled all over, I felt nurtured at the same time. I felt safe in their presence. Then I was lying down and they all came to me and picked me up. It felt like a lesson in COMBINED STRENGTH!"

"Listen for your needs and wants and give them to yourself. Anyone, no matter how hurt, can listen to themselves and take action."

"Change happens when necessary. Don't rush anything. When the time is right, all will align for change to happen. Stay comfortable within your skin and embrace each new phase as it presents itself. Love yourself enough to be patient."

"There is power in holding stillness inside until fruition. Then, like a fine wine fermented to perfection, power spreads out. Discernment is pertinent. Power doesn't get flung about hither and to and fro. It is used wisely. Gratitude is extended because no one *owns* power."

"How do you grow? At your own pace. You're the one who decides how fast and in which direction."

"There is no Path. There is only remembering. The 'Path' is whatever helps you remember."

May you value your thorns that protect
your most precious fruit.

ADDITIONAL MEDITATIONS & MOVEMENTS

SILENCE IN BREATH MEDITATION

This exercise is designed to help you focus on your mind through the calming power of your breath.

-To begin, find a place that is private and peaceful. It can be inside or outside. Keep any distractions to a minimum (phones, cell phones, kids, dog).
-Find a position that is comfortable for your body. Close your eyes and place your attention on your heart area. This can mean your physical heart or the general area of your heart, whatever feels comfortable to you. Breathe. Feel your chest expand and let go. Breathe in deeply and feel your lungs and heart fully expand. Hold your breath for a moment and then exhale, feeling it exit your body. If you notice your mind wander, redirect it back to your heart and lungs. Do not get irritated if your mind thinks of something. This is what the mind does. If your attention drifts, bring it back and breathe. Do this over and over. When your mind wanders, notice the thought and its subject (such as hunger, stress, worry, remembering) and then let it go. Bring your attention back to the breath. Resist the temptation to think of these feelings and thoughts as bad because they can be great illuminators. They can show you areas within yourself that need to be tended and refined as you become more comfortable with allowing your mind to be quiet.

-Do the above exercise for at least five minutes for a few days in a row. Continue to practice, even if you spend the whole five minutes bringing yourself back to the breath. If you find at the end of your five minutes that distracting thoughts or feelings keep you tense, take a moment and go into the thought or feeling that is distracting you. Is it anger, boredom, irritation? These distractors can help us find the places that are blocking us from being able to calm the mind. Looked at this way, they are, in fact, our friends.

-At the end of your five minutes, bring your mind back to your body. Offer gratitude to your body, breath, and any sense of calm that you experienced, if you felt that you didn't get an overt message. Write about this quieting exercise.

RIVER MEDITATION

Water is the essence of all life. In addition to this being true on the physical level, in many cultural traditions the concept of a river is used to describe aspects of our existence—the stream of consciousness, the river of thought, as well as the river of existence as a whole. You can draw on the image of a river in this meditation.

-A way to ponder your thoughts is to imagine a stream. Imagine yourself kneeling at its bank. Fix your eyes on the center of the water. You could imagine looking at the bottom of the stream, and then the surface. At some point, you might imagine a leaf comes into your field of vision while watching the water. Imagine this leaf to be a thought in your stream of consciousness.
-In this moment you have a choice. You can focus on the moving river and watch the leaf float through your vision, or you can focus on the leaf, grab hold of the thought and give your mental energy to it.
-In the river of your mind, your thoughts can be a distraction or inspiration. The practice of meditation is to learn the difference between the two. As each thought comes downstream you decide to follow it or stay in the calm water. It is up to you.

May the tumbling waters within you
bring clarity of calming vision.

TREE MEDITATION

-Imagine your center and then imagine yourself in a natural environment, any place that comes to you where a tree might be.

Breathe a few times and then let your imagination play... Feel yourself stretch to become a tree. Feel your feet become roots and allow them to sink into the Earth beneath you. If you're having trouble, imagine what it *might* look or feel like. See/feel your hair becoming branches reaching high into the sky. Your roots connect you with the Earth and your branches connect you to the sky above you.

-Allow the energy of the tree to move through you, from Earth to Sky. Don't allow any judging voices to grab hold of your mind. If this kind of distraction comes into your mind, start over with the intention to relax and feel connected to tree energy. Think of this as imaginative play, so there is no way to fail.

SPRIT WORLD JOURNEY:
Explore yourself as tree while listening to the drum. What happens?

CHALLENGE MEDITATION
Life challenges are not fun, but they are opportunities to hone one's spiritual skills. Experience does not mean that challenges are not experienced, the task at hand is to see challenges as opportunities to connect with centered Self and Spirit more deeply. You are invited to use the following meditation to help you find out more about a challenge that is troubling you, or one that needs attention.

-Sit with a relaxing sound, or in silence. Feel the rhythm of your breathing, and allow yourself to become calm and receptive. When you feel ready, think of a challenge that you face in your life. As you sense it, notice your body, heart, and mind. Allow yourself to feel the challenge, rather than think about it. Then ask yourself any of the following questions, listening inwardly for your feelings and answers.

-What feelings surround this issue?
-How have I felt about this in the past?
-How have I suffered by my own response and reaction to it?
-What does this problem ask me to let go of?
-What part of this problem must I learn to deal with?
-What great lesson might it could teach me?
-What can I learn in this situation?

In using this exercise to consider those things that challenge you, understanding and openings may come slowly. Take your time. Be kind with yourself.

SHAKE IT OFF MOVING MEDITATION
Find a private place to hake, hum, or rock in a variety of ways while listening to a piece of music that pleases you. For ten minutes focus on different parts of your body, and how these actions feel while doing them. There is no way to fail, and the point is to imagine shaking, rocking, humming out any energies that are not helpful, and to calm your mind enough to experience a mild trance during this meditation. Do it as often as you need.

To dive deeper, explore the Explore your Spirit World course:
weboflifeanimists.com/product/explore-your-spirit-world-course/
Coupon code is in end pages

May the sacred rain wash clean
the painful dust from your leaves.

Chapter Three
HEALING FOR OUR PAST

**Finding and tending wounds of the past,
to see what might be there.**

**It can be scary for those who look,
but to heal, one must dare.**

The word "Healing" carries many meanings and a lot of hope. Everyone wants to be healed from pain of all sorts. We want physical healing, emotional healing, ancestral healing and even, hopefully, species healing. We don't want to hurt, especially when we are not clear about why or how to heal the hurt.

On a personal level, healing can indicate that a physical ailment goes away. But even if it does not, other kinds of healing can occur. Past traumatic experiences can be tended, relationships can be mended, and inner balance can be found, especially in current stressful or challenging situations. Even our death is a sort of healing that waits for all of us. Oftentimes, "healing" looks different than we expect.

Since all humans are a part of the web of life, our personal healing experiences directly affect our relationships with our ancestry, community, species and all other species on this beautiful planet.

TRAUMA
Generations alive today are learning more about trauma every decade, how it affects us and how to heal from trauma stuck in our bodies. My current definition of **trauma** is as follows: Emotional and physical responses to a distressing, painful and/or disturbing experience that can cause long term effects on body, mind, soul, families and societies.

I am not an expert about trauma, in this text I speak of trauma from a perspective of "soul loss," "soul wounds" and "soul restoration" for personal and ancestral healing. I humbly offer these ideas for you to find what works for you.

Veterans after the war in Vietnam were the first to hear the term Post Traumatic Stress Disorder and since then, it has been acknowledged that responses to trauma are not a "disorder," but are normal. Most humans have experienced some of the many types of trauma. It seems that trauma is part of being a human, especially for those raised in a traumatized, and traumatizing, culture. The good news is that tending and healing trauma is possible with help.

SOUL LOSS
There may have been a time in your past when a part of your soul/spirit/essence/life force left, hid, was wounded or stuck because of a traumatic experience or era. You had to go on with your life, without an opportunity to acknowledge and process the experience. This can be called soul loss. If your body was physically hurt during the trauma, or purposefully traumatized by someone, you may have a soul wound that is still with you. These unexpressed pains can reveal themselves as you go through life, many times leading to feeling depression, anger, anxiety or physical ailments.

Soul restoration practices can help you find younger selves that have been hurt and are not fully functioning within you due to trauma experienced. Losses and wounds from ancestral or past life experiences can be worked with, retrieved and tended—years, generations or lifetimes after they began.

There are two general areas of soul loss/wounds experienced by many people—Multi-generational soul wounds inherited from ancestors, and those from trauma experienced in one's life. Soul restoration practices guide you within your inner world to recruit allies who can help you. Rhythms of rattle and drum can guide you to travel back into various time loops ("places" where your younger self is stuck) to find and connect with your younger self that was separated 10, 20, even 40 years ago. It is also possible to explore ancestral and past life experiences that are still negatively affecting you in this life. You have ancestors and allies in the spirit world who are perfect for this job. Call upon them, they will come.

HELP

Some soul restoration work can be done alone, using support tools (like this field guide), and other soul work is best done with a soul tending helper. There are practitioners who are skilled and trained in these areas of healing. Web of Life Animist practitioners are available, and other practitioners can be found in your community or online. See below for suggestions for finding a good fit.

May clouds, stones, birds and Earth speak as you shed your skin.

HEALING HELPERS

If, and when, you feel you need help, I encourage you to find someone that is qualified to assist you through any emotional healing that would be helpful to you. When help is needed, seek someone with whom you can feel both vulnerable and safe. Keep seeking until you find someone who is worthy of your trust.

I have included four things I learned from my own experience to keep in mind when seeking a Healing Helper:

1-There are hundreds of styles of counseling, coaching, body/energy work and therapy. Find a good fit by researching online, asking for referrals from people you trust, and be open to trying a few modalities and practitioners. If needed, always ask if a sliding scale is available. If not, can you afford it without getting in debt? If not, keep seeking.
2-It is important that your helper practitioner has an understanding of, and compassion for, your lived experience, especially for BIPoC,

LGBTQ+ or Military, and those healing from childhood and/or sexual trauma.

3-Find someone who shows confidence that you know what you need and that they are there to support your healing process. If you find that the therapist has the attitude that they know what is best and you do not feel listened to, move on.

4-It is important that you feel safe with the person with whom you are working. If a helper tells you or acts as if they are attracted to you, or they say things that make you uncomfortable for any reason, they are not the right helper for you. Move on and find someone else. Trust yourself and ask your inner guidance to be present with you as you find your healing helper.

For Animists and Earth honoring People:

5-You need someone who does not think that hearing voices (from trees, fairies, ancestors or guides) or having visionary experiences is a pathology. You need someone who understands aspects of Animism.

SPIRIT WORLD JOURNEYS:
-Ask for an ally to help you find an appropriate "healing helper."
-Ask for an Ally who can help you feel safe.
-Offer gratitude for all the support you have, and have received, in your life so far. Don't forget to include yourself.

*Some people have forgotten
the wisdom they knew,
then they forgot they forgot
and passed that on to you.*

*Trust you can remember
what will save you and your kind,
if you simply turn inward
and ask in your mind*

*"What am I ready to remember
To help me unbind?"*

A WAY THROUGH
Soul restoration includes the spirit world journey (discussed in chapter two), which can be used for any of the subjects discussed in this chapter. Please remember that tending your pains and forging a new path takes time. Patience and diligence are needed for soul healing work, but know that understanding can come, and healing can occur.

It is also important to know that by exploring these practices you may unearth feelings that do not feel pleasant, at least at first. This is not necessarily bad, even if it does not feel good. If you go on a spirit world journey to tend a painful experience and you come back with feelings that are uncomfortable, write about them, journey about them once again and ask for an ally who can help you with the feelings. If needed, do not hesitate to contact your healing helper or go to a helpful group for support. You are not alone.

SPIRIT WORLD JOURNEYS:
-Ask for an Ancestor who can help you retrieve lost and tend wounded soul parts when you are ready.
-Ask for an Animal who can be with you when you need courage.
-Ask for guidance regarding your soul restoration journey, as well as a team of protectors who have your back (imagine who you would feel safe to protect you).

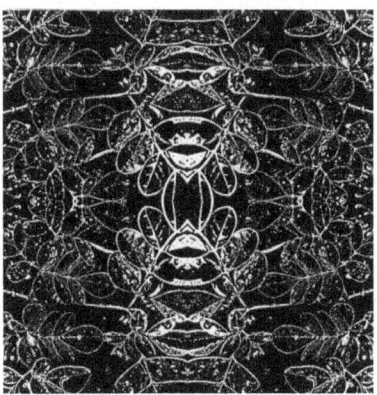

May the Plants of Life nourish you as you heal.

"Sometimes looking at ourself may not be fun. But it is a great gift. When we look at ourselves from our calm observer self we can see the things about ourselves that we want to nourish. We also have the opportunity to see those things that we can move through. Think of blocks as mental or emotional clouds that block your sunshine"
(Quynn's Journal, 1998).

HONESTY
It is helpful to decide to look plainly at our feelings, their perceived causes and the possible changes needed for us to heal. When it is time, we must be willing to look at our family historical trauma to understand our own story, so we can heal as much as possible in this moment.

SPIRIT WORLD JOURNEYS:
-Ask for a trusted ally who can be honest with you regarding what you need most now.
-Ask for an Earth honoring ancestor who can help you remember your sacred self.

THE PAST IS THE PAST

Due to events of the history in the last thousand years, our ancestors had to live lives that some of us can hardly imagine. Many ancestors experienced starvation, multiple plague sicknesses, and horrible deeds done by oppressive "others." To survive, people have learned to say, "The past is the past, it's over, forget it," but ultimately, this does not work. Forgetting something does not mean getting over it. Before we can let go of emotional pain, human beings need to unearth and process the emotions and feelings entwined with the experiences that caused it, because trauma becomes imbedded in our bodies, not only our minds.

Imagine your ancestors, depending on their experience, who lived in a state of trauma long enough that it made many impressions upon cells and souls of your kin. In some cases they began telling themselves, "This is how it has always been," and maybe even forgot that life could be another way. Yet we, their descendants, still feel the pain.

If we, the living people in our family line, have experienced trauma and pain for so long, passed down from generation to generation, then we can assume that our ancestral line has been "marked" by trauma. Said another way, our inherited cells have gotten used to living in a traumatized state. However, it is possible to tend and release the pain we carry from our ancestral lineage. At this point it does not matter if you believe that this is possible, just continue to hold on to your desire for change to occur. This is all you need for now.

"I started having thought voices tell me, "There is nothing wrong with you." With that idea echoing in my soul, my known world cracked apart and I began to understand and dismantle the dissatisfied and sad feelings I had felt for a very long time. I have worked on this for many years, with many healing helpers and many, many journeys. I am here to tell you that it can be done. If we listen, we can hear how to change our world from the inside out" (Quynn's Journal, 2010),

SPIRIT WORLD JOURNEYS:
-Ask to be shown a time when you were hurting, yet someone told you to "get over it" in one-way or another. As you remember that time, ask for an ally who is strong enough to help you soothe your soul parts that had this experience.
-Ask to be taken to an ancestor who can help you understand a pain handed down in your ancestral line. Know that you have all the help you need to reclaim your power from that ancestral pain, and yet there is no pressure to do it now.

THE GREAT FORGETTING?

During the time of Covid, past traumas have been re-activated in many people. It is important that as the influence of Covid-19 wanes that we don't just forget and try to shove all the untended traumas back into their boxes. Living through a pandemic, and all that it has brought forth, is traumatic. Yet, it has shown us individually and collectively where the traumas live in our lives, cultures and ancestries. It is up to us to not fall, once again, under the spell of forgetting, because in the long term, it does not help us.

SPIRIT WORLD JOURNEYS:
-Ask for an ally who has been supportive of you in the past.
-Ask that ally to show you a "spell" under which you are still living. Ask to see how a "spell of forgetting" has negatively affected your life so far. Know that you have allies and ancestors who are capable of helping you untangle yourself from those things that hold you back.

May the illumination of the sacred flame
guide you through dark times.

TENDING WHAT NEEDS ATTENTION

The process of healing is like traveling in unknown territory without a map. It can be exhilarating…and also terrifying. However, know that you have the memory of the map you need to guide you, in the cells of your body. You can weave your way through the stories, spells and feelings of your past and wind up in a beautiful place called YOU. Since I know how this feels in my own world, I will offer some ideas for you and your journey. Take what works for you, leave the rest.

When you feel ready to approach healing in an area of your life, begin to look for the root of the issue. Many roots are in childhood. Dealing with your early years can be a difficult task because remembering your lives so young may be challenging and relying on the memories of family members is not always helpful. It is delicate work, yet profound.

***Helpful Hint:** If at any point you read something in the following text and you have a strong visceral reaction to it, such as anger, sadness, nervousness, nausea…maybe you have some healing to do around that area in your life. Ask yourself, "Of what memory does this feeling remind me?" and let yourself approach it in your mind. Ask for a protector ally. Then, journey to that feeling, time or issue. If the feelings are strongly painful, seek out your healing helper or support group for assistance. Trust that you are both the "One Who Seeks Healing," *and* the "One Who is Already Healed," at the same time.

SPIRIT WORLD JOURNEY:
-Ask for an ally who can help you look at your childhood in a loving and protective way. Tell your inner world that you need loving attention from your allies around these issues. Ask for an animal who wants to be a strong protector of your inner child, maybe an animal that was present with you as a child, in your dreams or imagination.

A CHILD'S EXPERIENCE
Although there are no cookie cutter formulas for healing, over the years I have noticed a pattern. For many adults, their childhood experiences fall into one (or more) of three general categories, each with their own challenges surrounding the healing process. Please understand that the intent of the next few paragraphs is not to create competition about who has had the best or worst life. The purpose is for each person to learn how to look objectively at family stories and find the learning, and healing, in them. This is how we can eventually be released from the deep hold of emotional pain.

The first of these groups includes those children who know, without a doubt, that they are loved. They were told they were loved and there was never a question about that fact. This does not mean, however, that these children are immune from incurring soul wounds and/or loss. Personality disorders of one or both parents, addiction and trauma (such as divorce or death) cause pain that needs to be healed. Day to day trauma, as in dealing with a longtime addiction, can cause a schism in the minds of children who know they are loved, yet their parent(s) are not happy and well. Trauma can come from within the family, or it enters from outside the immediate family structure, but for anyone who experienced sudden trauma, it can change everything in the family, usually for the worse.

The second group consists of those children who were relatively sure that their parents loved them while growing up, but personalities between parent and child were so divergent, and expressions of love were warped or absent, that doubt was cast in the child's mind. These children may feel doubt that they are loved, or doubt of their own sanity in the context of their parent's world. The parent may mean well, but either they are not equipped to be a fully functioning parent (because their lives are so filled with sadness, pain or numbing substances that they are preoccupied with their own pain), or they did not really want to have a child in the first place (consciously or subconsciously). People who have experienced this family reality can easily doubt their own reality due to the doubt that was formed early in life.

The third group consists of those children who experienced direct and overt physical, sexual, verbal and/or psychological abuse from parents or caregivers, or they were disbelieved and not supported when they told their parents about such abuse by close others. There are many hellish ramifications from having to experience abusive trauma as a child, especially by one or both parents (or the ones that are in the role of caregiver). The cycle of abuse can follow these children into adulthood, making their lives a maze of unsatisfactory relationships and self-doubt, addiction or repeated violence towards others or self. This is obviously the most difficult experience for a person to heal, but it can absolutely be shifted over time with persistence, patience, courage and help from one or more healing helper.

Almost all children have experienced some form of trauma that stemmed directly from one's upbringing, which stems from the way one's parents were raised, and their parents before them. Very few of us did not experience anything painful. If you are one of these people who escaped unscathed, count your blessings. For the rest of us, we must think of fixing our "damage" as we would think about fixing a car. When our car breaks down, we do not think of it as weak, stupid or evil for not working smoothly and efficiently. It is not useful to think of our car as inherently bad. Of course, this may seem obvious, but when an aspect of our life breaks down, it is easy to feel that something is fundamentally wrong with us when we are unhappy, angry or feeling "broken." If only we would give ourselves the privilege of treating our emotional and soul wounds as we do our car when it needs a tune-up, our healing process would go much more smoothly. Feeling that something is inherently "wrong" with you is a tool of colonization.

"When I find a place within myself that feels hurt, I try to immediately feel compassion for my pain and attempt to understand it, rather than judge or condemn my feelings. This is not an easy task, so I ask for help from my spirit world. It has taken me many years of practice to remember to do this. In each moment of pain, it is up to us to remember

to love ourselves, to accept ourselves, to be patient with ourselves and to ask for help from our Spirit Allies." (2013)

EXERCISE:
Take a few breaths and allow yourself to feel or think about your childhood. The good and the bad. Notice the places that feel like blank spaces in your memory. Imagine that you can connect with your child self at various times in your childhood, and when you feel ready, ask for an ally to help you seek out your multiple childhood selves at these different ages, as if you are calling to them from all the hiding places where they are in your inner landscape. Imagine that you can tell them how special and loved they are, even if you doubt it. You are the responsible, loving adult they need now. Breathe with them for one minute. Then write about how you felt during this exercise.

SPIRIT WORLD JOURNEYS/JOURNALING:
-Imagine a sacred location in your inner world or your childhood past that can help you process uncomfortable emotions related to your young years. Ask to meet your protector for this place.
-Imagine in this scene a place where you can cleanse or transform any feelings that cause discomfort from your childhood. You can imagine a burial site, a fire pit, a washing pool where you leave your feelings for processing. Ask your protector to watch as you do this sacred work.

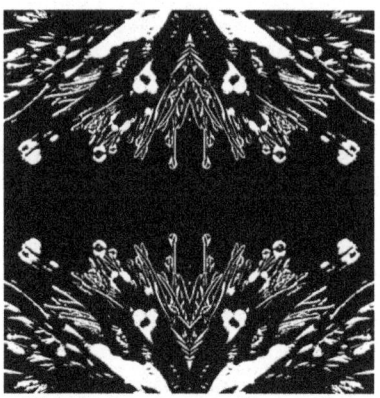

May the dew drops on Pine needles
show you facets of other worlds.

AREAS FOR HEALING: SAD TIMES
I would imagine that each of us, if asked, could remember a time in our past when we were (and may continue to feel) sad. It is difficult to say why one sad experience or phase affected us until the present, yet every person has memories of sad times that no longer affect them.

Childhood trauma, body image, gender, sexuality, friendships and betrayal can leave a blanket of sadness in adult life. We, with tools and helpers, can hold space for our younger self within to acknowledge, admit, accept or release something from their life experience, which is in our past. Over time and with attention, our younger selves, and our adult self, can create more space for healing in one's life.

SPIRIT WORLD JOURNEY:
-Allow a sad time in your past to come to mind. How would you change the scene so it was no longer sad? If you were a magical being with many powers, what would you change? Who would you ask to come to protect you? Imagine that scenario, even if it feels like imagination. Ask for an inner healing helper to come and help you talk with your inner child who was sad. What would you say to a child who was sad? What would you say to your inner child?

AREAS FOR HEALING: "BROKENESS"*

The colonized cultural story that we have inherited is that we are broken, flawed and filled with sin. Depending on the particular version of the story, we all get the message at some point along the way that there is something wrong with us. This is a story.
It is not truth.

*I put the word "broken" in quotes because I hear many people refer to themselves, or times in their life, as "broken." I do not believe anyone is broken, and yet, I honor the word "broken" as a common way to acknowledge how feeling that something needs to be "fixed" can lead us towards wholeness and healing. The guiding light can come in through the cracks.

QUESTIONS TO PONDER:
-When were your "broken" times? What caused them?
-How were your parents able to parent you? How not?

-Have you ever gotten sick as a result of stress? If you are not sure, note when you have had significant health problems (physical breaks and sickness included) in relation to stressful times in your life.
-Do you numb yourself to deal with stress or trauma? Have/Are you partnered with someone who does?

SPIRIT WORLD JOURNEYS/JOURNALING:
-Where do you feel the most emotion while writing your answers to the previous questions? Listen to music/rhythm and ask for an ally/mentor who can help you regarding your emotions and body responses to any of the above questions. You might ask, "What do I need most right now to help me tend these feelings?" or something similar.
-Is there a part of you that is stuck in one of these times, that is ready to come home to you? Ask for help while listening to the drumbeats. Trust that help waits for you.

AREAS FOR HEALING: FEELING DIFFERENT
Many have experienced trauma from continuous experiences of being different than the status quo norms. Bullies and tormentors leave unseen scars within sensitive and "different" children. These traumas from childhood often go untended until much later. Many sensitive children of Earth have experienced some version of feeling different: "too big," "too small," "too dark," "too weird," "too plain," "too gay," "too much," "too *something*." Sometimes being different is considered "strange," "quirky" or "crazy," and sometimes it is dangerous.

QUESTIONS TO PONDER:
-How/when have you felt unaccepted or ridiculed growing up?
-Do you see similar patterns as an adult?
-How, and where, have you felt like an outsider or different?
-To what degree (on a scale of 1 to 10) have you healed these feelings?
-Have you ever used substances to ease self-consciousness or depression? How do you feel about these experiences?

WRITTEN EXERCISE:
Write your thoughts and feelings about the above questions. No one will see these pages, so write your deepest feelings and thoughts, no matter how "pathetic," "sad" or "strange" they may seem to you now.

SPIRIT WORLD JOURNEYS:

-The pain of feeling different, less than, or too much can be difficult to tend. Before you go on a tune in or journey about these feelings, please create a superhero guide as your helper. Let your childlike imagination create the perfect hero for this kind of job. Don't hold back! When you are ready, ask for your super powerful guide to be with you. Ask them to show you a "different" time in your life that is ready to be visited.
-Insert yourself and your guide into the scene (or as close as you feel comfortable) and ask what needs to happen in this journey. Know that you can rework any situation and make it different. Know that your adult journeying self can talk to and teach any character in the journey, including your younger self.

May the Water Springs of the Earth
remind you of your healed Ancestors.

STORIES OF ANCESTORS

"Our NOW was created by the belief system of the repressed, unhappy and toxic culture of our forefathers" (Quynn's Journal, 1993).

One of the most important things that people of our time need to do is to address our ancestral past. For many people today, family history is painful to some degree. For some, they have experienced personal pain inflicted by one or more family members or caregivers. For others, their heritage has been traumatized by injustices caused by the colonizing and oppressive cultural system. Due to both reasons, humans now have a genetic memory that is fragmented, confused and still in pain. We, as individuals, now have the power to stop this cycle in our own bodies and minds, as well as in our families and communities. To achieve this, each of us must gather our courage and decide to overcome the paralyzing feeling that there is nothing we can do to change. It is, indeed, time for change.

CAREGIVERS, PARENTS, GRANDPARENTS
For children, adults are the Gods and Goddesses in human form. Each child grows up believing that their parents and caretakers have elements of Gods and Goddesses within them. A child needs to see these adults as caring and strong. If one is lucky, this is the story of your childhood. If this is not the story of your childhood, luck is still with you.

There is so much that we inherit from our parents, and that they inherited from their parents. Many in colonized cultures might immediately think about material objects or wealth that have been (or will be) inherited from parents or grandparents, but I am referring to deeper inheritances. You and I inherit our ancestors' experiences, feelings, wounds and triumphs. They become embedded in our cells, in our beliefs and in our bodies. Whether spoken or not, we are acting out (consciously or unconsciously) aspects of our ancestors. As we decipher what is "us" and what is "them," each can learn to see the stories as opportunities to heal your lineage, and it begins with you.

Unfortunately, some will never be able to completely come to terms with their mother and/or father figures in physical life. Death, distance, danger or differences may keep a full emotional reunion from happening. In these cases, I wholeheartedly encourage you to go on with your healing. In addition to the helpful effects of feeling connected in your Animist practice, there are many forms of therapy that can be utilized even if you cannot work directly with your parents.

One thing that helped me in my healing was to realize that I could have all my anger, pain and resentment about what I didn't get from my mother and father, while also feeling compassion for them as people having to live through the traumas they experienced.

MULTIGENERATIONAL TRAUMA
So much trauma has occurred through within human populations that at this point it is in everyone's cells, memories and bones. Our personal healing journey must include our ancestor's healing as well.

Vulnerability, honesty and accountability are necessary companions for this challenging yet essential work. After many generations of having to suck it up and "deal with it", now is a good time to begin to unpack and heal it.

For half the human population, women and girls, patriarchy has created multiple dangers for too many generations. Today, at this writing, women and girls are still fighting for, and losing, human rights around the planet, including in the "land of the free". The collective trauma is impossible to deny, and many ancestresses (in the physical world and beyond) have much healing to do. You can help yours and they help you release and empower what is needed.

For anyone with African and/or Indigenous ancestors around the planet, the traumas from colonization and systemic oppression are calling for justice and healing. Ancestral lived experiences are witnessed and soothed by descendants' loving attention.

For all who have any amount of European ancestry, most were originally persecuted Animists, while some were the persecutors from the beginning. Since Europeans spread around the planet, whiteness was created to colonize the world. An important part of ancestral healing involves addressing wounds of the soul, and all European people have wounds created from perpetuating, supporting and benefitting from violence against "others" all over the planet. If this idea creates discomfort, sit with it, don't push it away.

However hard it is, and however long it takes, tending to the wounds of our ancestors is so important, for individuals, families, and communities right now. We need collective ancestral healing.

QUESTIONS TO PONDER:
-What contributed to your mother and father's pain?
-What stories were told about your parents and grandparents?
-Did they have access to Education? Power? Freedom? Joy?

WRITTEN EXERCISE:
Write to, or about, each of your parents (that you will not send). What needs to be said about your relationship with, or perception of, them? Even if either or both have passed, were not present, or there is purposeful distance, write what you need to express.

SPIRIT WORLD JOURNEYS:
-Ask for help in your healing and offer gratitude for your life.
-Imagine yourself as a peacemaker, a diplomat, a messenger, for your ancestral line to deliver a message, or to do something that is much needed by your ancestors.
-What message do you need to hear from your ancestors?

May your flowery blooms be nourished
by the power filled Sun.

"It has happened again. I step through a door into being able to feel so much raw emotion. It is so strong it is almost painful" (Journal 1996).

HEALING WITH KINDNESS
Many people have an idea that going to a counselor means that you are "broken." I don't think of it that way. If you want to learn something new, you find someone to teach you. If you need a coach, you find a coach. If you are unfamiliar with something, you are smart to find someone to help who is familiar with the subject, right? If you are unhappy or depressed or angry, and you want to find a way to change that, you may need some assistance. Effective emotional healing helpers are out there. If you feel you want or need one, it is possible to find a good match for you. Assistance is not always or only in the form of individual therapy. You can receive help from books, support groups, movies, and classes, and of course, practicing the Animist arts.

When we feel pain, our instincts tell us to find a way to avoid it. Yet, we cannot go around our pain or skip over it to get past it. We must go through it in our own time, in our own way. One aspect of healing is to be able to hold space for the grief lodged in the body, mind and spirit. Expressing and releasing grief is an essential part of healing. healing is a place to intend to travel through, not a place to make camp forever.

WRITTEN EXERCISE:
Write about your experiences with healing so far in your life, as well as two areas of your life that could still use healing.

May the sacred fronds of the Cedar tree
teach you what they know.

A HEALING NOTE OF POSSIBILITIES

The past can tell you where and from whom you have come, but this time requires us to look forward. We are standing on the cliff of a new possibility for humankind. There is much wisdom of the past upon which we can rely, and we do not have to do things the way they have been done in the past. Our parents and grandparents, and those before them, did their best with what they had available to them. Oftentimes, that was not much. Our ancestors were colonized, and some more than others in our lineage have been the ones perpetuating colonization upon others. We must create new paths for going forward because colonized people and systems have caused so much pain to Animist Peoples, as well as other Beings of this beautiful Earth. While school history books tell us that western culture is the height of civilization, there is much happening today that our descendants will call barbaric.

The healing referred to in this chapter does not intend to forget, condone or erase the pain of our ancestors, or the pain any of them inflicted on others. As we move towards a more just and equitable future, we must go through this challenging terrain as individuals, because it is important work that contributes to our collective process of moving beyond this current era of greed and imbalance.

I encourage you to continue in your quest to tend that which causes you pain. These tools can help you help yourself so that you can cultivate beauty and power in your life. Whichever tools you choose to use, the most important thing to remember is to be kind to yourself, especially when you feel vulnerable, "less than" or unheard.

-Your expressions of grief, healing and beauty are important.
-You are invited to be creative and compassionate with yourself.
-Your commitment to decolonizing your Self is a gift to the web of life.

During and after Covid times, there is much pain, grief and real reasons to feel vulnerable. If you feel stressed, confused, anxious and/or angry, you are not "broken". These are natural responses to trauma, and what we are all going through is certainly traumatic. Call upon all who have been helpful to you in the past, and any new allies and ancestors who are waiting to help.

EXERCISE:
Ask for a protector ally who can introduce you to Grief. You could see Grief as a monster, or maybe that Grief is a guide, a healer, a teacher for you. Imagine that Grief knows you well, and loves you. Grief has a message or a gift for you right now. Ask what it is and then listen.

To dive deeper, explore the Soul Restoration course.
weboflifeanimists.com/product/soul-restoration-healing-course/
See coupon code in end pages

May the oldest Maple trees shield you
when you need it most.

Chapter 4
CONNECTION WITH SACRED PLACE

I am the acorn meant for the worm
The bird dream beak full of squirm.

Purrs the cat, faster than flight
Not a thought for the coming of coyote night.

Rain turns into rabbits and pups are born
Or drought turns to hunger and traps are worn.

Every strike by lightning or blast by wind
Gives an acorn a chance to sprout once again.

Will the deer keep the wolf at bay?
Will the sapling survive the cubs at play?

Hundreds of years an oak may grow
With treasures & secrets, remembered by crow.

The Peoples of Earth see beauty and strife
and we are all a part of the web of life.

"Each of you has ancestors that lived with the Earth and knew the ways of 'magic'. They are in your DNA. Call on them and ask them to whisper to you. They will whisper to you what to do in these times."(in a vision 2000)

RECONNECTING

During this era of lingering colonization, oppressive white supremacy, rising fascism, rampant capitalism and pandemic sickness, there is a deep collective longing for a sense of reconnection to the Earth and our Soul. As we learn to tend the disconnected places within ourselves, we are more able to feel the natural connection with the world around us. Colonizers, fascists and capitalists do not generally see the Earth as sacred, but to be an Animist is to be in relationship with the other humans and beings other-than-human who are also on this beautiful planet. This chapter considers "Sacred Place", which starts in your heart and then extends outward to encompass all that surrounds you. May you explore these connections with an open heart.

SACRED SPACE

"Sacred" refers to anything that is important to everything else. It is needed by Creation. This being the case, then Sacred Space is technically everywhere. The Earth is sacred. You are sacred. The fly buzzing around your head is sacred. We all live together in the web of life. When we become quiet in our heart, we can more easily hear the voices that make up the sacred community of Life around us so we can tend to our mutual needs. If we are going to find our way through coming challenges, we will do so through our collective connections.

EXERCISES:

-For anyone who lives in a place not of your ancestry, that was stolen from the original inhabitants (specifically in the lands now called "The United States" or "Canada") take a moment to speak the name of the Indigenous Peoples where you are at this moment, and where you grew up (if different). If you do not know who the original inhabitants are, search for a map online.

-Notice where exactly you are in this moment and offer gratitude for this sacred place. Your body, the air you are breathing, the place you are sitting or standing (what is this place? Is it a room, or outside?). Now expand your awareness out further...to the town or region where

you are, to the continent, and then the Earth. Notice which "places" you feel more connected to than others, or which places feel more sacred to you. Offer the most heartfelt gratitude to any space that you felt hesitant or resistant to consider sacred.

May the feathery crystalline blooms
of your DNA sing joyously.

WISDOM IN YOUR BODY

We begin with your body in this chapter because the dominant culture feeds all with negative messages about the human body. The culture in which we live seems obsessed, yet uncomfortable, with the physical body. To those influenced by monotheistic religion, the body can be considered dirty or even an impediment to being "pure." Although you may not feel this disdain, you have likely been affected by these unhelpful attitudes. The body holds much wisdom and knows the healing that is needed. It is important to listen to these messages.

You could imagine your body as an antenna that is constantly picking up and sending information. You can remember how to use this information for your health and safety. Your body is an emotional antenna, as well. Almost everyone can tell when someone is mad, sad or scared. The ability to perceive emotions is an ancient survival skill. The more you know about your world inside your skin, the more you will be able to safely move with the flow of the web of life. This is the ultimate survival skill.

WRITTEN EXERCISE:
-For one day, up to one week, keep track of all your gut feelings and what happened in each situation.
-Take note when you feel an "ahhh!" moment of clarity or recognition. This feeling is an indicator of a message from your body wisdom.
-When was the last time you went against your body wisdom? What happened? Do your best to release regret or shame about not listening, and instead, just observe.
-Next time you feel inner guidance, listen.

You are the center of your Universe. Where you go, your center goes. Even if you do not feel centered, your center is with you. Feeling centered in your body is the foundation of feeling connected with, and a part of, all the other beings who live on Earth with you.

"When I first visualized my center, it felt as if I had a black cloth draped over it. I could perceive light behind it, but my center felt sad and asleep. I practiced connecting with it, and slowly the blackness began to part. Eventually, I could feel my heartbeat in my center (which I could never do before) and over time, with practice, I felt a stronger connection to my intuition" (Journal 1996).

EXERCISE:
-Close your eyes and turn your attention inward. Feel your breath in your body. Notice if you feel any voices or sensations of disregard or judgement. Guide them to step aside. Breathe, and when you are ready, feel for where your "center" is located within or around your body. (This is not an exercise to "think about" your center, feel it.)
-Allow your attention to focus on your center, wherever you feel it. Breathe into it. How do you sense it? Can you imagine it, feel it, hear it? Offer it gratitude in some way, and notice if and how it (and you as a whole) shift or change during this process. Sit a moment with your center. Then, as you begin to bring your attention back to the world, let your center know that you are listening to it.

FEELING YOUR ENERGY CENTERS
There are many cultural ways to describe our energy centers within and around the human body. Keep any system that you resonate with, and for now please imagine that you have eight hoop-like disks spinning through and around your body in varying places. Think of the first one

as spinning around your feet. The second one is spinning around your knees. The third one is around your pelvis/hips. The fourth spins around your waist. The fifth circles your heart and the sixth spins around your throat. The seventh spins right above your eyes and the eighth spins around the top of your head. Imagine these areas of energy spinning around your body.

Sensing these spinning hoops of energy is helpful because each of the places where they spin is important to your entire energy system. Each place holds together vitally important organs, ligaments and hormones that need to work together to function properly. The more you listen to them, the more connected and balanced you will feel within your body and the world around you.

EXERCISE:
-Imagine each area of your body as described above, one by one. Feel what it would be like to have a protective, healing energy field spinning around each area.
-See if you can make it spin. Which way does it spin? If you can get it to spin both ways, how does it feel to have it spin one way, and then the other?
-Play with letting each area spin in color. What color do you feel/see for your throat? What color do you feel around your pelvis? You may have heard about a particular system that says this area is associated with a certain color but let the area of your body tell you what color it is that day. How vibrant is the color? If it does not seem as bright or strong as you would like, adjust it so that it feels better to you. How might you do that? (Creativity is helpful here.) The colors that come today might be different tomorrow.

BODY TRANCE
Consider trance as a sacred act of communion. What is trance? Combine repetitive movement and/or sound with an intention to let go, or loosen, the logical mind. The human ability to create this state is ancient and it is helpful for our body, mind and spirit. When we carefully encourage trance, we can be more open to the wise guidance of the Universe and the natural world. However, since the dominant culture teaches that trance is bad or dangerous, it is desirable to learn to let go of those assumptions. Our bodies don't have to be taught how to experience trance, they only need to be reminded.

Each of the following forms of trance can be done in simple and private ways. Find what feels good to you.
-Dancing, rocking, swaying, singing, toning or humming
-Shaking the body in simple ways (however feels good to you)
-Breathing (you can breathe deeper, faster or slower than normal)
-Making rhythmic sound (clapping, tapping, drumming, rattling)

EXERCISE:
Find a private place and practice each trance method for 5 to 10 minutes. What do you feel?

As we hone our ability to connect between our inner and outer "worlds," we can begin to extend our awareness to our cycles, timing and connections beyond our skin.

PERSONAL CYCLES
The human life cycle has rhythms and these rhythms have shifted over time. For example, before the industrial revolution spread through communities all over the world, most humans lived with the cycles of the seasons—planting in spring, harvesting in fall and resting in the winter. Today, many live in a world of work and commitments that are clock and calendar related and usually don't honor or allow for times of rest or reflection. Your own rhythm may not be in sync with your commitments and you may end up ignoring your own rhythm, in order to keep up with your life. Listening to your personal timing rhythms can help you make choices to honor your Animist ways as you live your life in the culture of clocks and day planners.

As a specific example~ The time Covid brought on the "Great Resign", when a large number of people realized that their "job" was not nourishing, or even worth showing up for, and so they (you?) resigned. May you be able to shift parts of your life to be in alignment with your natural timing.

EXERCISE:
-Find three ways that you could make small (or big) changes in your life that honor your natural rhythms, either in physical ways (like changing a commitment) or emotional ways (like releasing guilt about

not liking something or feeling hesitant to make your needs known). Notice how these changes affect your wellbeing.

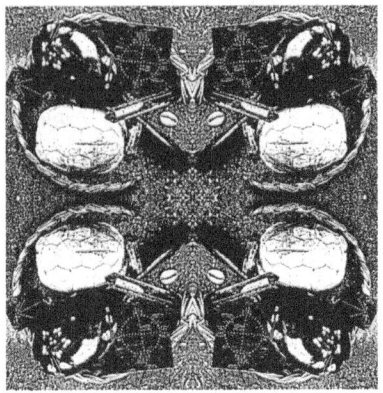

May your Earth altars include and honor
what is most important to you.

AN ALTAR IS A PORTAL

An "altar" is one word for a physical focal point for an idea or belief, where love and intention can be expressed for a time. Everyone has an altar of some sort. Many have family pictures arranged on the wall or on a shelf. Others have a place where they keep special items that remind them of meaningful times or as a dedication to their divinity. In the process of recognizing and acknowledging sacred space around you, an altar is a wonderful creation. You can have an altar in your car, workspace and in your home. It doesn't have to be fancy or large. As with many aspects of spiritual life, what is important is the sincerity of the attempt.

Think of your altar as an expression of you, as well as what and who you aspire to be. You may find a picture that expresses your feelings of who you are or who you are becoming. You can place flowers, water, an offering of food, a candle or incense to your altar. It is helpful to tend this space to keep it fresh and up to date with your current prayers/intentions. When you get a feeling your altar needs a cleaning, or even that it is ready to be dismantled or changed, listen.

EXERCISE:
In a space that you feel to be "home", even if it moves with you, pick a place to become your altar space (This space may be moved as

needed). Offer gratitude for the blessings in your life and create your altar to reflect what is important to you right now. What you create is your sacred practice, and it can look how you want, and contain what you need.

WRITTEN EXERCISE:
Did you grow up seeing, or interacting with, altars? Do you have an altar space now? Write about it.

TIMING

Timing matters. Any of us could have every intention to do something, start something or end something, but if the timing is not right, it is unlikely that what is wanted will work out as expected. Sometimes things fall into place and the timing is perfect. Other times, the timing is "off" and things stall, or fall apart. When this happens, it is a good time to pause or stop to reassess. Timing has its own language and can seem magical in its synchronicity and outcome. It is up to each person to sense and follow one's own timing, and this requires practice.

WRITTEN EXERCISE:
-Write about a time when you wanted to do something and the timing was just right.
-Write about an instance when the timing was not appropriate for what you wanted.
-What did you learn from these experiences?

CIRCLES

The circle is a sacred shape found again and again in the web of life. At all times you are connected to the circle of life on Earth and beyond. As you cultivate your gifts and learn to trust your inner knowing, you increase your capacity to feel the ways in which you are connected in this sacred circle.

To think of a circle in a more personal sense, you always have the right to create a sacred circle or sphere around you that protects you. It is also helpful to build a circle of friends/loved ones whom you can call upon. You also have a circle of other-than-humans that you can call upon for the support you need in the physical and spiritual worlds.

There are times in life when it can be helpful to "call a circle" by deciding a ritual, a healing circle or sacred gathering is needed, and then taking actions to make it so. To "open" (start) your ritual you might invite the directions, your spirit guides and ancestral allies to assist you. You can then "cast" the shape of a circle for protection by creating a circle in your imagination, drawing a circle in the dirt on the ground or constructing a circle of crystals, stones, candles or other items. At the completion of your ceremony or gathering, it is important to "close" the circle, to release those allies you asked to join you, and to end the connection between worlds. There are many ways to call, open, cast and close a circle, but what is most important is to focus your intention on your need, ask for help from your allies and ancestors, and offer gratitude in a heartfelt manner.

EXERCISE:

-Notice the number of circle shapes around you. Look deeper and you will find more.

-Imagine a circle you would like to call for a reason that is important to you right now. Think of at least one other kindred spirit person you would like to invite to this circle, whether it's in person (if safe), online, by phone, or even in thought. If, and when, the feeling is right, invite them to "sit in circle" with you. If you do not feel comfortable asking another human, you can call a circle with a dog friend, ancestor, your child self, or an imaginary friend.

EXPANDING YOUR SACRED CIRCLE

Being connected to your body helps you expand your awareness beyond your skin, to listen to and learn from the sacred world around you. Your circle expands and includes many allies in the physical world. Trust that your circle is strengthened by your relationships with the other sacred beings of this amazing Earth (and beyond). The rest of this chapter explores these connections between you and the world.

May your Roots be linked with all other Beings.

YOUR PLANT AND ANIMAL CIRCLES

"I just had an experience. The trees around me caught my attention. They told me they want me to stay with them for a while. They said that they are sad because people don't talk to them, or even notice their beauty as individuals. They said people don't understand like they used to. They want me to honor them, to notice that no tree is exactly like another. All are individuals and I should treat them that way, with the awe that inspires. This would make them very happy. They said they would tell me things in exchange" (Journal, 1996).

Wherever you live, you are connected to the plants and animals who live around you. They are a source for great power, whether you live in the wilds, the suburbs, a trailer or an apartment in a big city.

PLANTS

We depend on plants for nourishment. We eat them, they feed animals that many eat, and they produce oxygen and medicine for all life. While plants are stationary and seemingly quiet, they have their unique gifts to share with us. Their many shapes, flowers, and colors make our Earth a beautiful place to live, and we cannot live here without them.

Plants are beings with their own wisdom and ways. Listen and watch them to learn what they have to share with you.

EXERCISES:

-Which plants do you eat? Which are your favorites? Tell them, "Thank you!"

-Go outside your dwelling. What plants are immediately outside? Look at them without judgment or prejudice. Next, look at the plants within 25 feet of your front door. Even if you do not know their names, how many different plants do you see? Don't discount any!

-Say hello to at least 3 plants closest to your door. If you don't know their names, see if you can identify them. Send your telepathic mind out to them and thank them for their friendship. Ask them if there is anything you can do for them.

May you have the pleasure of sitting with an elder Tree.

TREES

Trees are wisdom keepers. Most were here long before we were born and will remain long after we leave our physical bodies. Their roots extend into the soil, their trunks and leaves are present here with us, and their branches reach up to the sky. The "Tree of Life" is an important symbol in many cultures because trees share so much of themselves with humans, including the oxygen they exhale.

EXERCISES:

-Look around your home. What is made of wood? Notice all the forms of once living trees you live with in your home.
Offer them gratitude, your tree friends.
-What trees live closest to your home? Learn their names and tell them thank you from your heart. Notice if one tree stands out to you. In your

mind, ask that tree to be your protector and helper, and then imagine that you are breathing with that tree.

ANIMALS

We share this beautiful Earth with our animal kin. While some humans have animal friends (dogs, cats, etc.), we all are related to the many animals living their lives near us, whether we notice them or not. Our collective human experience is connected with those of hoof, claw, shell, fin and feather. The animals spin and keep the web of life intact. We need them and they need us to protect them. It is our jobs to be advocates and protectors for those who are endangered, and for all who are suffering due to climate change, forest fires, drought and human encroachment. Prayers, donations and actions are necessary during this time of climate emergency.

EXERCISES:
*-Do you eat animals? Which ones? How do you honor these animals?
-What kind of animals do you see in a day, a week? Write them down along with any associations you may have with them. Also, take note of synchronistic interaction with any animals. Notice if you judge any animal "better" or "less than" the others. Offer all of them gratitude and protection.*

CONNECTING WITH NATURAL TIME

In addition to connecting with the physical world around you, it is important to look at the concept of "time." The way we have been taught to think about time is limited and unnatural. There is an unfortunate history of the clock and "mechanical time" as an instrument of colonization, which I address a bit more later in this chapter. However, since multidimensional time is one of the essential elements of this reality, it is important to inspire you to explore "natural time".

The movements of the stars, sun, moon, flowers, tides and seasons flow in their own rhythms. Each has its own calendar. Our Animist ancestors not only relied on these cycles for their lives, they learned how these alignments indicated when a perfect moment was occurring. Planting, harvesting and migrating all have their own cycles that help people live and flourish in their environment, for those who know how to read them. You have this wisdom too.

WRITTEN EXERCISES:
-Earth/Sun/Moon cycles do you follow?
-Notice the natural cycle pattern in your life- Think of them as wise elders and write a poem or letter to honor them.

May the sunrise and clear sky
greet you after a challenging storm.

THE SEASONS
Knowing the seasons where you are is necessary knowledge and it is a wonderful way to feel the relationships between our Earth, Sun and Moon. Cultures around the world mark their seasons differently because weather in various bioregions have different cycles, and yet there are often many similarities between them. While the northern and southern hemispheres experience summer and winter at opposite times, we all experience some version of winter, summer, autumn, rainy and dry seasons. Each season has its wisdom and challenges, and in recent years the seasonal effects of the ongoing climate emergency have increased dramatically.

EXERCISE:
Notice the flow of the seasons where you live now. Which is your "favorite"? What do you like about each season? What are the significant changes where you live?

COMPASS DIRECTIONS
East, South, West, North, and the points in between, create the circle of the compass. Four compass points (also called the four directions) are important because they orient us to where we are in the physical world.

Every Earth-honoring culture honors the directions in some way, whether they call it "East" or "the place of the rising sun". Directional awareness is a needed skill for humans living in the physical world. Not all cultures agree on the attributes of each direction, such as associated elements or animals, so if you do not have a system already in place for your practice, you can learn about various ways cultures address the directions, and you can also create your own descriptions as you feel them.

EXERCISES:
-Apply the compass points to your home.
Which way is North? East? etc.
-Close your eyes and think of one of the directions. Ask within, "What color do I think of when I think of this direction?" Then let one appear. Ask this question as you think of North, South, East and West. Please note that these color associations do not have to be written in stone, you can choose colors for now.
-Go to your chosen altar space, find a piece of blank paper, draw a circle with each direction marked in the color that you chose for that direction. Now, from your sacred space, find North and orient North on your directional map to the Earth's North, then fill in the other directions. Post this map in a prominent place so that you will always know your direction when creating sacred space. What do you associate with each direction and how you flow through the directions (NSEW, ESWN+).

ELEMENTS
All of Earth is made up of multiple elements. There are the 118 known elements of the current periodic table. In many Animist paths, particular elements are specifically called upon and honored in life, and in ceremony. Oftentimes, the following are highlighted and called upon (although others can certainly be included): Air, Fire, Water and Earth. There are many personal and cultural ways to call upon and honor them, and you can have your own too.

EXERCISE:
-In your own way, connect an element with a direction. How do you feel they go together? Does Earth go with North, or maybe Water with East? Different cultures pair different elements with different directions, but what do your pairings look like? Find associations that feel good and true to you.

WRITTEN EXERCISE:
-Research similarities and differences among cultural opinions about the directions and/or elements. Which descriptions resonate with you? What are your choices in your tradition?

May you dance the rhythmic cycles of the Moon.

PHASES OF THE MOON

Our planet is in a dance with our moon that affects the entire Earth and all of us on it. The moon has been with us since the beginning of human time. There are many cultural stories about the sacred relationship of Moon and Earth. You have moon honoring ancestors in your lineage, so connecting with the moon phases (New, Waxing, Full, Waning) each month can help you explore the phases, emotions, and patterns of your personal and ancestral relationship with our moon.

THE MOON IN US

The moon phases have lit the night sky and tracked time for all who live here, and moon's gravitational pull affects everything on Earth, including birds' navigation and migration, ocean tides, weather, the hours in our days and the shape and tilt of our planet.

The water in all of our bodies is affected by the moon's pull, and of course, mature female humans bleed through the menstrual cycle in a pattern that mirrors the 28 day moon life cycle. As women become elders, the bleeding stops and a new relationship with the moon is forged. No matter our gender, our human emotions are influenced by moon's phases, especially the full moon. Even when it cannot be seen due to trees or clouds, it affects our inner waters, our whole bodies and our moods, and is a sacred part of our physical world.

EXERCISE:
-Think about the various stages of the moon and what they might mean for you. Many feel that the full moon is about expansion, illumination and fullness while new moon is about introspection, planting, healing.
-Use these ideas or come up with your own and find a way to honor the two nights of each month when the moon is at its fullest and quietest. You can do this alone or with others in any way that you want. If you cannot see the full moon from where you are, know that it is there behind the clouds, trees or buildings, always looking after you.

SOLAR CYCLE & 8 DAYS OF THE YEAR
The current timing system by which many humans live our daily lives is the Gregorian calendar, which is synchronized with very little in Nature. It does follow the solar year, but it is not in rhythm with Nature's timings.

This calendar was invented by Pope Gregory XIII in 1582. Paired with the clock, together they have spread this unnatural system of "time" throughout the world.

There are a variety of ways to evenly divide a 365-day solar year. Two examples are 13 months of 28 days (commonly described as the moon cycle), as well as 15 months of 24 days (360 days, the degrees in a circle) with 5 days left over, equaling 365 days.

Whether you count a year as 365 days, or 360 days (plus 5 days to reset), our Earth year is one cycle around our Sun. As our Earth moves through this cycle, there are honored times that mark the change of seasons as our planet tips toward and away from the Sun. While the seasons vary depending on the particular location (latitude and hemisphere) of any Earth place, all cultures acknowledge the shifts in seasons because they affect all life on Earth.

One way to honor these seasonal changes in this yearly spin is through designated days—the Summer and Winter Solstices mark two seasons of the year (most light and most dark from the tilt towards or away from our sun). The halfway points in between them are often called the Equinoxes, which mark the times of balanced light and dark (and tilt of Earth) in Spring and Autumn. Additionally, there are four midpoints between those four, in early February, May, August and November. These eight days a year have different names and are honored in different ways by people all over our planet. The cycles are opposite in the southern and northern hemispheres. The cycle of Life flows through the seasons each year, and human cultures honor these times.

EXERCISE:
-Track these days in your year and explore ways to acknowledge the change of seasons in your life.
-Learn about the Gregorian calendar and how it has spread around the world, as well as how it factored into colonization.

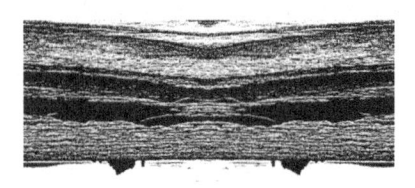

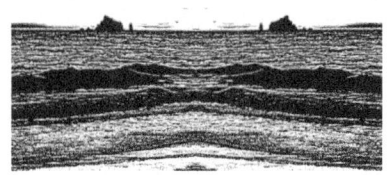

May the Ocean waves share their patience with you.

OUR GREATEST TEACHER

"I have had to listen to Nature to find out who I am and where I come from" (1999).

The Earth, that which we often call "Nature," is the combination of every part of the web of Life that sustains and teaches us. For anyone who says, "I know Nature, I love Nature, I hike and camp and recycle…" This is not what is being addressed here. It is important to set down the colonized idea of knowing Nature intellectually, especially thinking that Nature is "out there", something separate from ourselves. The path to reconnection is to allow the insulating bubble that "protects" us from the "wilds" of the natural world to melt away. Being colonized is to be afraid of our wildness and the wilderness of the world. Do not be afraid of your wildness, it has much to teach you.

The following exercise is included both for meditation purposes as well as to guide you to "listen" to places that call you for deeper connection.

EXERCISE:
-Find a place outside of your home that feels comfortable to you (a place where you can close your eyes and feel safe). Look for a spot that draws you to it. It may be the base of a tree, in a field, on a secluded bench in a park, your backyard, on a cliff in the forest or looking at the sky in the middle of an urban jungle. When you find a spot that speaks to you, greet it and begin to slow your breathing. Breathe.
-Relax into the sounds, smells, and feelings of this place. Close your eyes and listen to it with your body. If a thought comes, notice it, and allow it to pass. What bird sounds do you hear? Do not resist human sounds—relax into them and listen to all the life that is there.
-Do this exercise for 5 or more minutes, and then thank this place. As you depart, leave no trace of your visit.

EARTH KEEPER

You can connect with the Nature around you because Nature is everywhere and ultimately Nature is all of us together. Clouds, Plants, Trees, Water, Animals, Wind, Dirt and Stone—All can teach meaningful lessons (both amazing and challenging), nourish body and soul or annihilate in an instant.

All Animists are Earth keepers and protectors, and it is important to remember that Earth is not a "thing" to be consumed or used by humans, "it" is an incredible gathering of sacred beings, all living together. Humans are but one People living here on Earth, and all the other People have a right to live, and flourish, here too. You know this already, now it is essential that we all act on it.

In 2021 the climate crisis has evolved into the climate emergency. The time is now to quickly grow in our collective understanding about how the Earth systems are changing. All Earth Protectors must continually ask, "How can I be helpful?" and then listen for guidance about how to proceed.

May our hearts, minds and actions remain open and courageous, guided by sacred ancestors as we advocate and protect our web of life.

May the Trees who shed puzzle pieces leave guidance for you.

To dive deeper into this chapter,
explore the Nature as Teacher course
weboflifeanimists.com/product/nature-as-teacher-28-day-animist-course/
See coupon code in end pages.

Chapter 5
GETTING ANSWERS

How can you tell the world is talking to you anyhow?
You know when you've been
wondering a particular thing
and out of the blue the answer sings?
From the mouth of a friend,
or a page in a book.
There's the answer, plain as day,
without having to look.
That's part of the fun in talking to Spirit,
as well as the gift.
You get to listen to the world,
look for Spirit in the world,
no matter how hard you resist
the idea that the world does guide us,
if we open and allow it to be.
You see, when we need help
we ask, we beg, we pray,
but then don't think we're heard.
But if we know we are heard,
and act that it's so,
then we know, to listen.
Listen to Spirit on the inside,
learn to recognize the gift.
A whisper in the ear, a nudge in the heart,
so easy to miss.
This is where it begins and ends.
This is where Life is, my friends.

"Most of what I am trying to do in this lifetime, I've done before. I just need to remember how to do it. It feels like I'm remembering bits of a dream, but the rest hasn't come yet" (Quynn's Journal, 1996).

TALKING WITH THE WORLD

All humans are born with an innate ability to ask for help in multiple ways. As we mature, these sacred abilities are naturally expanded, even when we are not taught how to use all of them. One thing we do learn is that when we need answers, confirmation or insight, we ask for help from our divinity, angels, our ancestors even luck... whoever we think might be able to help. From an Animist perspective, all beings in the web of life are alive and therefore can hear the pleas for assistance. It is possible to receive help and guidance from the living world when you need it, even in ways you do not quite understand or believe.

This chapter offers stories and ideas for how you can recognize and strengthen your relationship with your intuition through dreams, divination, synchronicity and the ability to sense messages within the web of life. As these connections are enhanced, your communication gains clarity.

YOUR BFF, "INTUITION"

Each person is born an intuitive, sensitive being who is connected to the worlds of synchronistic flow. Intuition can be thought of as a muscle, which is only strong when used and that atrophies when ignored. Most people have been made to doubt their intuition at some point in the past, but the relationship can be repaired and enhanced.

Intuition is so close to us, so natural, that often we do not notice it. Once we do realize that intuition is something real and we begin to believe we have it, then it calls to us more strongly. Your intuition is your friend, mentor and ally, so when you sense its presence, say hello.

EXERCISES:
-Keep track of all intuitive hunches for one day, especially the ones you tend to ignore or discount. Take note of how often you follow them and how they play out.
-Note where you feel your intuition in your body. How do you feel it? How does the feeling vary in different situations?
-Thank your intuition every day for at least one thing, whether you feel it or not.

WRITTEN EXERCISES:
Write about the role of INTUITION in your life.
Some questions might include:
-Do you trust your intuition?
-What were your parents' attitudes about intuition?
-Think of at least one time when you honored your intuition.
-Think of at least one time when you did not honor it. What happened?
-Do you have any fear about connecting with your intuition?
-What excites you about connecting with your intuition?

THE POWER OF YOUR DREAM WORLD
"I feel so...so many things, beautiful, strong, amazing things. I am being taught things in the hours before waking. This morning they were powerful teachings about humility and power. I know what I'm being taught as it is happening, but when I wake the actual teachings are too far in my brain to remember. Though, the information is blending into me and my body remembers" (Quynn's Journal, 1997).

Animist cultures have always trusted in the prophetic and informative nature of sleeping dreams. Some believe that the dream world is the "real" world and the waking world is the construction of our dreaming mind. Dreams are a gateway to realms that have been accessible to humans since the beginning of our existence. A dream can bring a message from your personal and ancestral soul. The dreaming mind is a powerful teacher and guide.

There is an entire language of dreams. The symbols, the images, the hidden meanings can be confusing or cryptic, but assume they come as helpers, teachers and messengers. Even scary dreams, if not feared but faced, can bring forth helpful insight and guidance. In dreams you can fly, share telepathy, and the rules of the physical world do not apply in the same way. No matter how often or profound the messages, your dreamworld is a "place" to be understood and honored.

*May your dream nest rest within the protected
gateways of antlered wisdom.*

COURTING DREAMS

If you want to enhance the possibility of remembering your dreams, try one, or all, of the following exercises to find what is helpful for you.

-Keep a journal at your bedside. As you wake from a dream, write it done. Remembering a dream can be tricky. If you move too much, if you open your eyes, if you put your feet on the cold floor, a dream could be lost. It is easy to think that you will remember a dream without writing it down, but much more difficult to actually do. Write down what you don't want to forget.

-If you must wake up with an alarm clock, and you would like more opportunity to remember your dreams, set your alarm twenty minutes ahead, then hit "snooze" so that you wake up more slowly, hopefully catching a dream in your mind.

-If you wake up in the middle of the night, do not turn on bright lights. If you want to remember dreams, or be able to go back into one, keep your sleeping area as dark as is comfortable. If you want to write down your dreams at night, use a low light or write in the dark.

-If you are pondering an issue, write your question in your journal or on a piece of paper and put it under your pillow to ask your dream world for guidance. Then write about what comes forth before, during and upon waking from sleep.

-When writing, don't worry about penmanship, spelling or grammar—just write. Also, do not censor what you write.

-Assume that your dream world is trying to communicate with you, and it is up to you to learn *how* your dream world speaks to you.

ARE YOU A DREAMER?
There have always been people who have been known as "dreamers", those who receive information and guidance in their dream state. If this is you, please give your ability to dream the respect it deserves. Being a dreamer is not always easy, as you may experience dreams that are challenging or confusing. Not all dreams you dream are for or about you. This ability has always been revered and feared in human communities because of the powers they hold. In your dreams, if you receive messages for others, prophecy, foretelling or connections from beyond the grave, you aren't crazy, you are called "dreamer".

EXERCISE:
-Offer gratitude for the dreams you receive (especially challenging ones), ask for instruction, clarity and information when you need it.

DREAM BLOCKERS
There are times when people consciously or unconsciously take actions to block the dreaming process. This is understandable, and yet the dreaming mind is doing a job for you, so blocking it might inhibit aspects of your life. I list some common dream blockers below. Notice if any sound familiar.

-Disbelief in the power of your dream world will hinder your ability to receive guidance from your dreams. So, first and foremost, believe that dreams have power and that this power can help guide you.

-Emotional and physical states, such as stress, exhaustion or depression will usually hinder a dream message (sometimes, however, these "altered states" can actually induce dreams).

-Alcohol and a variety of medications can make you sleep so heavily that you do not remember your dreams. There are many people who have painful dreams, so they take medications (legal or illegal) to purposefully keep their dreams at bay. If this is you, please remember that in the long run, if you are able to heal the pains that cause bad dreams, they can dissipate. Pharmaceutical medications only suppress them. Plant medicine teachers may help blend the dream and waking worlds, yet they can make it harder to night dream.

"You must remember! Everything you need to know is there. You just need to open yourself to it" (Spoken in a dream, 1991).

INTERPRETING DREAMS

Sometimes, the message in a dream is crystal clear. Other times you may wonder "What in the world did *that* mean?" Learning to decipher dream meanings is a practice unto itself. It can be tricky to ask others to interpret a dream for you. One person's, or even a culture's, interpretation of a dream or dream character may, or may not, be valid to your particular dream. Be open to what the scenario or character might be saying to *you* regarding *your* life. Even though you may not understand a dream now, the meaning may be revealed later.

If you have a dream that stays with you, ask yourself many questions and then listen to your intuition. "What was the dream telling me?" "Who does this dream character represent?" "How did I *feel* in the dream?" "Help me understand!" These are good beginnings. Journeying or meditating on the meaning of a dream can also be very helpful.

May the bones of our ancestors
nourish the blooms of our NOW.

GUIDING DREAMS

Many people have experienced dreams that they consider guiding dreams. This is an important job of the dream world, to guide us in this life. I have included a handful of my own guiding dreams here so you can see how my dreaming mind has communicated to me in the early years of my path of becoming kindred with Earth. The number in the parenthesis is the year of the dream.

~A long and detailed dream. First, I was at a reunion of people that went to my high school who were three or four years older than me. I felt inadequate and unsure of myself. I can't remember who I was with, but she kept embarrassing me. Then I was in the desert. I was thinking, "There is somewhere I need to go." There was a snake to my left by my ear. He was dark red and thin. He started whispering answers that I needed to know, even though I hadn't asked exact questions. Then he said, "You have a beautiful body." Then he held his head about three inches over my body. I was very nervous because I knew I had to be still. He was very powerful. Then he was on my right side, telling me things again. It was beautiful. He was blessing me. The dream ended when I found myself at a social function with a lot of wealthy people, and I felt very self-assured. (1991)

~I was walking out on a jetty and I saw snakes right by my feet. They weren't attacking me, they only struck when I jerked away out of fright. In the dream I thought, "I wonder what would happen if I could stay calm and not be afraid?" I had no more scary snake dreams after that realization. (1994)

~I dreamt that I had HIV. I was flabbergasted. I felt that all that I was doing was for nothing. I was in many social situations but I was looking at them differently. Even more profound than me having HIV was that I thought "Great! All this is for nothing—
I don't have much time left, so what should I do?" I knew I wanted to stop doing what I was doing for work, and I wanted to get out of debt. What would I do with my time left? Travel and work on my unconditional love of others. The overall feeling was that HIV was a symbol. The underlying message was,
"Do what you would do as if you only had a short time left."

Last night I asked to see what would happen in my life in the next six months and then this morning I had the dream. (1996)

The dream above ended up being a guiding dream. Within nine months, I had changed my life and began the life that I now live.

~I dreamt of an amazing being who appeared in the backyard of my childhood house. She had a horse's body but could sit back on her hind legs like a rabbit. She was a beautiful brown and she was my guide. I was with two other people and we were getting ready to go on a journey, so I needed this guide. Then I saw a caravan of people who looked like they were in a circus, and we were told we were to "travel and share with others what we had learned." I had the sense that this was in the "after times," although I did not know when that would be. (1997)

This dream has stuck with me all these years. It feels like my strongest guiding dream. The horse being was the one who helped me learn how to journey down the tunnel I later saw in my mind. I feel we have entered the realm of the "after time."

~I had to undergo an initiatory test in the dream world. I was going down a tunnel and then I was wearing a blindfold. Then I was in a room with a light on me (an interrogation room?) and a being asked me things like, "Why are you here?" and "So, you think you are ready for this, huh?" I knew I was going to have to prove myself. I thought that there was something about journeying for someone else that was a new level for me (I had been asking for guidance about journeying for others).

~He then blindfolded me and sent me into a forest. I was put through some confrontations with menacing animals. I thought with my thinking mind that this initiation should be frightening, but I felt a solid, comfortable feeling in my gut. Pretty soon, I figured out that this was the message—to experience the solid feeling of calmness. At one point something confronted me and I remembered the feather I was holding and I held it up. That got me through the test. Then, when confronted again, I remembered my staff in my physical world and I grabbed it. Realizing I could do this made me feel more confident. Finally, the male being that was blocking me stepped aside and I knew that I had passed.

I started to walk past him and then I turned and asked if he had anything for me. He gave me five white stones. (1998)

DREAMING OUR WAY FORWARD

As a human species, we dream our way through life. Generation after generation, people have dreamed in every language and for every reason. Our collective consciousness is expressed to and through us by our dreams. Even when we do not remember our night dreams, humans have the ability to connect to our dreaming mind through other methods, including many practices in this book. Intuition, journeying, divination, synchronicity, visionary experiences, meditation and trance open our inner portal and guide us to connect with the web of life.

EXERCISE:
-Call up a meaningful dream to journey about it with drumming or some other repetitive sound. Call upon an ally to help you remain protected during this process and hold the intention to learn more about the dream. Find a way to change the dream in a way that feels helpful to you.

May the Birch Goddess bless you
with divine understanding and insight.

THE ART OF DIVINATION

Divination is the act of consulting the world around us (the spirits, our guides, ancestors etc.) to help find answers to dilemmas that may be beyond our rational minds' ability to understand. This is an ancient practice. People around the world have used bones, read the cracks in shells, thrown I Ching sticks, read Tarot cards, watched clouds and animal tracks…there are so many ways tune in. Every culture has had a way to consult the spirits, and you can find yours.

While divination has been a part of every human culture throughout time, for many recent generations, divination was a serious crime in Europe and in the cultures that Europeans colonized. It was thought of as a "conversation with the devil" that was harshly banished. This has caused fear of divination to remain in some people today. You may have family members who feel this way, and maybe a part of you has been conditioned to feel this way as well.

EXERCISE:
-Ponder your relationship with divination to this point in your life. If you have felt resistance, hold the intention that you can address the reasons why with journeying, meditating and through divination. If you do not have a divination system to work with, you might keep your eye out for one that you like, and you can begin your relationship.

THE QUESTION

In my experience, the question is the first half of the power of divination. I have seen many people miss out on the positive potential of divination by how they ask their question. Here are some glaring examples: "Will I meet my soul mate?" or "Will I be successful?" My answer is always "I don't know, will you?" Then I ask them to change their focus, instead of thinking "if," think "how." Such as, "What do I need to do to find my soul mate?" or "What can I do to help my business be more successful?" or even "What am I not seeing that may be blocking me from experiencing love?" These questions give you an opportunity to have a conversation with the divination so you can get practical information.

For the most part, asking "yes" or "no" questions severely reduces the possibility for a meaningful answer to emerge (unless you are using a pendulum, which is specifically for a "yes" or "no"). It is generally more effective to ask about the best possible way out, or through, the situation at hand.

Here are some examples of useful questions, depending on the issue:
"How will (blank) affect my path?"
"What is (insert a name)'s motive?"
"Why am I feeling sad?"
"Where am I on my life path right now?"
"What comes if I tell (name) how I feel?"
"What is the most important thing for me to focus on now?"

You do not have to ask one, and only one, question. A divination's response to a question often leads to another question. Yet, only ask one question at a time. It is easy to mistakenly ask multiple questions. For example, "What will happen if I move to San Francisco in January and take the new job?" This has three questions within one question. If all three questions were asked together, you could receive a muddled answer and then become confused. Instead, you can ask first, "What will happen if I accept the new job?" Then, "How will living in San Francisco affect my wellbeing?" Finally, for advice about the timing of the move, ask about moving in the particular month being considered.

Ask questions of your divination system until you feel that you are finished, or until you get a sign from the cards (or the bones, sticks, etc.) that the session is over. If one too many questions has been asked, you may receive an answer that is obviously off base. This is a sign that it is time to stop. If instead of feeling complete, you feel confused, then stop and listen for your next question, based on what has come before.

THE ANSWER
The answer is the second half of the power of divination. The first thing to remember is this: Just because you do not understand (or like) the answer, it does not mean that the answer is wrong or worthless.

Most people ask questions about the future, or how their present actions will affect their future. If, when you ask, you receive an answer that is confusing, ask for more clarity and consult again. Still confused? Ask the question in a different way or ask why you do not understand. If you are still befuddled, tuck it away in your mind and trust that your spiritual teacher (the energy that is using the deck) is trying to pass you a message that you cannot understand at this time.

When you receive an answer that feels confusing, take it as a compliment. Assume that you are in some form of initiation in your life. There is something to figure out, a puzzle that can only be put together by you. Also, know that the answer that makes everything click into place can only come when all the pieces of the puzzle fall together, and this happens in its own time.

If you get frustrated because you do not understand the answers or you are not getting clear or relevant answers, meditate or journey on the issue. Quiet your mind and ask why you are not able to understand. Ask to be shown more information in dreams or in your waking life. Sometimes you might receive clear and direct assistance and, other times, clues are given for you to find on your own. Either and both ways, trust that you are guided along your path.

CREATE A DIVINATION DECK:
-Cut a piece of paper into smaller pieces, with all being the same size. You could cut it into 6, 9 or 12 pieces. You could cut up a second piece of paper to have up to 24 pieces.
-On an additional piece of paper, write words that feel important to you (such as confidence, love, determination, satisfied, etc.). Write one of your words on each piece of paper. Now you have a divination deck with however many cards you just made.
-Shuffle the cards while pondering what to ask about. As you ask a question that has meaning to you, pull out a card and look at the word. Notice what comes to you. If that card leads you to another question, ask and pull out another card. Ask and pull until you feel the inclination to stop, or until you have an "answer."

ENHANCING DIVINATION SKILLS
There are thousands of types of divination used by people all over the world, all are designed to communicate with the living world. No system is inherently better than others, so find one or more that intuitively speak to you. You may be attracted to the pictures or the language or you may be drawn to a system because of the cultural affiliation, such as the I Ching (China) or the Runes (Norse/Celtic). The way to enhance your relationship with divination is to practice, practice and practice some more.

EXERCISE:

-Explore a variety of divination systems to see which forms and styles you prefer (you can do this online without purchasing anything). Notice which images, methods and stories that draw you in and make you curious. These systems are the ones to learn more about and ask them to talk with you.

-When you decide to work with one or more, consider your chosen ways of divination as new friends. Trust them, talk to them, ask for their advice. If you don't understand their advice, ask another question.

May your wishes and prayers fly on the wind
to where they can grow.

SYNCHRONICITY

As you awaken to the living world within and around you, you will experience synchronicity more often and you recognize it as a form of guidance and/or communication. Webster's Deluxe Unabridged Dictionary defines "Synchronize" to mean "to move or occur at the same time or rate; to have the same timing; to be synchronous." It defines "Synchronous" as "happening at the same time; occurring together; simultaneous." To be synchronous is to be in the same timing as another entity, occurrence, person or event. To be synchronous is to be human.

Every person has had experiences with synchronicity. This is how the Earth and the Universe guides and supports us. Unfortunately, some cultures discount the power of synchronicity. Instead, these experiences are described as "fate," "chance," "coincidence" or "luck". If we learn to ride the synchronistic wave, we have a better chance to be in the right place at the right time.

This assistance is available to all people when it is needed most, but you do not have to wait until a crisis shows up. You can cultivate synchronicity by learning to listen to your intuition more intently. When you feel that your gut is speaking to you, teach yourself to pay attention. Open yourself and ask for a clearer connection. Ask, "What are you trying to tell me?" Hold tenderly the attitude that someone or something helpful is trying to speak to you. Once you understand and recognize synchronicity, you will be able to see messages in events that at one time would frustrate you. An example would be saying to yourself when delayed, "I will assume this red light has prevented me from getting into an accident further down the road."

Look for the following clues that synchronicity is happening:
-Things can disappear and reappear in seemingly strange ways. When looking for something and you cannot find it (and it was RIGHT THERE!) or something totally unexpected shows up "out of nowhere."

-Unlikely strings of events. For example, you wake up in the morning and the first thing you hear is someone speaking on the phone who says "Lighten Up." Then, later in the day, you walk around the corner and there is the same phrase printed on a billboard ("Sometimes, you just have to Lighten Up"). Then the next day, a friend recommends a book about the same topic ("Ten Great Ways to Lighten Up").

-Repetition of symbols. You may continue to see the same symbols, animals, numbers or images in sequences. When you do, notice what you were thinking, doing, deciding.
-Many things coming together in one moment. Imagine going somewhere and three other friends (all of whom you were meaning to call) show up at the same time without planning to meet, and maybe without any prior communication.

Synchronicity is occurring all the time.
We observe synchronicity when we need it, but we can remind ourselves to see it all the time.

I have noticed that synchronicity in my life seems most present when I need it most. I see it as a way that my helpers assist me when I either don't know what to do, or when what is needed requires another person, and they show up at just the right time (like in the story above). Sometimes, I am tempted to send away synchronicity because it comes in a form that I do not recognize, or that a part of me wants to judge it as unsatisfactory. I bring this up because sometimes help comes in a way we need and not in a way we want. Many times, we are given just enough to do something, even though we think we deserve more. Trust what is given. This will lead to a stronger alignment between you and synchronicity.

An example from my own experience~
My companion got a flat tire when we were traveling through a town unfamiliar to us. He was fumbling with an inferior jack to change the tire. We both noticed a broken-down car in the same parking lot where we were trying to change the flat. Five minutes after beginning to get frustrated by the rusted jack, a car pulled into the parking lot. A man and woman got out with a top-of-the-line jack and started working on the broken car next to us. I asked them if we could use their jack. I found out that this car had been sitting in its place for a year and they arrived at that moment to fix the tires so they can take it home. Of all the times for them to decide to come and change the tires to take it away, they chose that day and this time. We had the tire changed in minutes, easily and gratefully.

THIS, OR SOMETHING BETTER
When we need help, we are usually in a vulnerable position. It is easy to take the first thing offered or to leap before we look. Only you know if the proposed thing feels right, so it can be helpful to pause, calm any worry and ask for clear guidance.

I work with the following principle. If synchronicity happens and something is presented to me, I notice how I feel in my body. As I ponder the decision, I note if I have a 100% feeling of "yes" in my body. It does not have to be an ecstatic yes, just a calm, confident one. When I practice this exercise, if I ask within and do not feel the "yes," I pass or get more information. I say to my allies, "This, or something better," and trust that if I pass, a better fit will come.

FEELING BLOCKED
Sometimes, synchronicity can come through what you perceive as a negative or stopping experience. Many times, for synchronicity to happen, we need just the right circumstance, *at just the right time.* Sometimes a perceived block might be indicating that is not the right time or place for synchronicity to happen. One of the most important things this path in life teaches is *patience*, the ability to wait for just the right thing at just the right time.

EXERCISE:
-Next time you experience synchronicity that leads to a positive or protective experience, express gratitude in some way. Give thanks for being in the flow. When we receive a blessing, it is best to recognize it.
-Think about the last time you felt blocked from something you wanted. Use meditation, a journey, or divination to learn more about why the block occurred and what there is to learn from the experience. Express gratitude for insights that comes to you.

May those who live in Ocean waters
live fully and beautifully.

SENSING IS IN OUR NATURE
Each of us are a part of the immense and intricate web of many beings in many forms. We are all connected in so many ways. One way that we are connected is that we can, and do, have synchronous interactions with Animals, Plants and Elements of our beautiful Earth. There are infinite ways and times when our paths cross in the physical world with a bird song, a bee's buzz, or a wind at just the right moment. These

awe-inspiring interactions can bring clarity, calm, sacred confusion, a message when needed, or as a lovely surprise.

There is also a form of communication with all in the web of life that happens during our sleeping dreams and with our visionary mind. Beings of this world and beyond bring us messages, interactions, teachings and initiations through our dreaming mind, both while awake and asleep.

EXERCISE:
-Think about times in your life when an interaction with animals, elements or plants brought you a message or insight that surprised or made an impression on you.
-Take note of a dream or visionary experiences you have had with other members of the web of life in which we exist. Offer gratitude for connections you have felt.

WHAT IS A MESSAGE?
If you are thinking about something meaningful to you or you make a decision and, for example, a bird "caws" right over your head...is that a message? A confirmation? A warning? If you find a feather at a perfect moment, is it a sign? If an animal crosses your path or you see an animal in your dream, and then you see the same animal in your waking life, what might that be saying to you?

There are many beliefs about what means what, but ultimately it is up to you to decide the meaning of messages. I am no expert about interpreting messages, but my lifelong practice has shown me to notice each time something synchronistic happens, offer gratitude, and go with what unfolds from there, moment by moment.

WRITTEN EXERCISE:
-Note when a synchronistic message comes from the natural world. What were you thinking or doing when it occurred, and how did the message come to you?

May the Sun, Flowers and ancient Saguaros
bring contentment to your heart.

WE ALL BELONG

This chapter has shared a few ideas for communicating with the world around, and within, you. I encourage you to hone your intuitive communication skills so you can assess what you know, know when to be where and sense when to do what. There are as many ways to be in synchronicity with the living world as there are people, and yet all varieties, methods and modalities have many of the same elements within them. When we need help, support, insight and answers, it is so helpful when we have tools to engage with the questions we have in our hearts.

The importance of your reconnection with your intuition, your inner world, the world around you and the energy that moves through all goes beyond your individual life. As you reconnect to, heal and embrace your authentic self, you also influence family members and people in your life. Cultures are created of individuals and communities, so as a culture, as more of us remember how to listen within and to the world around us, we can intuit answers to questions that need to be asked. These answers can help us do what needs to be done to support the collaborative and beautifully diverse life on Earth.

To dive deeper, explore Your Spiritual Tools course:
weboflifeanimists.com/product/your-spiritual-tools-course/

See the coupon code in end pages.

May you sense what is helpful
and discard or transmute what is not.

Chapter 6:
RHYTHMS OF FEATHER AND SMOKE
Self-Care for Sensitive People in an Unsensitive World

The wisdom is simple,
The message is clear,
You are a part of the world, my dear.

THE STORY BEHIND THESE RHYTHMS
I wrote this chapter as a separate small book in 2010 after learning that one of my younger cousins committed suicide. He was in his 20s and he was a sensitive being. Today he would likely want to be called "they", and would be considered "neurodivergent", "empathic" and "queer". This harsh and unsensitive world did them in, and they left this world hanging in a tree in a public park, their favorite escape place close to their mother's suburban apartment. I share this sad story because their death prompted my writing of the following chapter. I wrote what I wished I could have shared with my cousin.

Colonized patriarchal culture is dangerous to so many of us who are kindred of Earth, we all need practices for self-care, as well as shared stories that help us dismantle the spells of colonized mind and the aloneness of a sad heart. You are important and needed here. My hope is that the ideas in this chapter, and field guide, might help you trust it.

OUR ANIMIST CORE

We, as humans, are an equal thread in the amazing web of life. We are one species on this beautiful Earth, here with so many others. We are in relationship with the beings that animate this world, as well as the worlds beyond the three dimensions, and we can be in communication with all. Rocks, wind, plants, a mountain, all animals, the ancestors, even your car, all have an energetic essence, and all can, in their own way, communicate. Messages of communication from the living world can come through signs, omens, dreams, intuitions, visions, symbols and patterns. Animists also know that "life" is beyond the linear concepts of death and time, and we are a part of that web as well.

There are many people who might be considered an "Animist in waiting". This is one who is ready to remember their Animist understanding that has been seemingly frozen underground, waiting... Once activated, there is no more time for waiting. In their own time, their authentic self rustles awake, and their intuitive abilities are ready to be guided and cultivated. When it is your time to remember, it is to everyone's benefit that that you learn how to hone these abilities.

THE WAY OF CHANGES

The collective memory of our DNA remembers the melting of the last ice age 10,000 years ago like it was yesterday. It remembers asteroids, floods and catastrophes, and how one might feel the rumble of a waterfall way before one can see it, right now your DNA may be telling you "honey, changes are coming!" Change can come in many ways. In addition to Nature's kind of change, there are also changes caused by humans. Life-changing change can come in a moment, and sometimes (like now) we are the resistant frog in a slowly boiling pot of water.

Change has always been a part of life, so what can be done? Whatever kind of changes come around the bend, the most important thing to do is intend that you are in the right place in the right time, rather than the wrong place at the wrong time. Your intuition may save your life someday. It saves you every day.

AT HOME
The multidimensional nature of reality and the living worlds of Earth are very much alive, and they are capable of speaking to anyone who will listen. As we claim our Animist nature, it is correct to acknowledge that we each are "Indigenous" to Earth and we naturally hear the Earth speak to us. Many who read these words might not be affiliated or registered with a particular Indigenous nation, but all initiated Animists, registered or not, have an indigenous heart. For those who have forgotten, it is time to remember.

Our Animist nature is perfectly designed to help us communicate with the lands around us, and practice being respectful to other life forms, even if our overall culture did not teach us appropriately how to be in union with the web of life. If you are coming home to the realization that you are an Animist (whether you call yourself one or not), then it is a perfect time to listen to the land and spirits of the place where you live. Offer gratitude and make offerings. Ask permission from the ancestors of the land where you are and take action to protect the nature beings who live there. If your ancestors are not native to the land where you live, who is? Learn and acknowledge the People who have always lived there. Where do your ancestors come from? Honor them and that land as well. All is sacred and we must treat this Home with respect.

WE ARE THE ONES
We can receive messages from the living world because we are all made of the same basic materials, arranged in what scientists call DNA. Animistic cultures, especially those that have always used plants as spiritual teachers, have known this for thousands of years because Nature itself told them. For those of the Forgotten Peoples (those who have been made to forget our Animist nature over the generations), we are just beginning to fully remember that our DNA connects us to the living world, and these connections are now explored by those who study the sciences, as well as spirit.

The path is there. The tools are available. When each Animist in waiting decides to jump in, know that you can swim. In the stream of Animistic inner reality, you can even breathe underwater.

May the unfolding waterfall of Reality
embrace and nourish you.

REALITY IS NOW 2.0
We can imagine that humans have always wanted to augment, or
enhance, our reality. Our ancestors of old, the Animists of the world,
had access to a fantastically augmented life experience! When we hear
remnants of stories and see the art of these people of the past, they
reflect how often and easily the worlds blended and synchronicity
happened in their lives. People shapeshifted, danced and tranced, and
spirits became manifest. Something in them knew how to activate these
amazing feats. We know too, yet we have been made to forget.

In the recent past of humanity's long lineage, the great body of
knowledge about how people can naturally augment our own reality
has been suppressed, lost, burned or forgotten, but now humanity's
desire to experience the multidimensional nature of reality can no
longer be blocked. In scientific, spiritual and intuitive ways, people are
exploring expanded abilities of perception for the various senses to be
expressed through inner and outer technological means. The internet, 3-
D gaming and expanding holographic digital worlds, are all examples
of the beginning of a new era of human existence, for those who have
the hunger to play in the 'digital otherworlds', and who can afford it.

Whether this expanded external technology comes from our human
imagination, or we are getting a little help from our friends from the
future, no one alive today can deny its power to connect and enhance
our lives.

While the human population's thirst for technology is expanding at breakneck speed, Animists know another reality. Yes, personal and collective technology is the wave of the future, yet each of us still has the natural ability to augment our inner reality using our open mind and multifaceted spirit. Through rhythmic actions, altered states and a focused intention, we have access to many realities inside and around us. The living world has taught people how to perceive the subtle and expanded energies of the world around and within us since the beginning of human time. Ask for guidance and we will be shown what to do.

MEMES VS GENES
Meme= A self-replicating behavior pattern that moves through a population and determines cultural expression.

Whatever happens over the next 10, 100 or 1,000 years, the most important cultural seed to save for a balanced future is the meme of Animistic living. The meme of monotheism may or may not make it through, but whoever makes it through must ask and intend that the prominent meme is to live simply, with respect to others, and that humans remember how to live with respect for the changing Earth. The meme of Animism has the best chance of surviving when each of us is careful to not be engulfed by anger, resentment, despair or rage, as all these emotions contribute to our individual and collective destruction. Our mission is to be guided to be in the Right Place at the Right Time, with the Right Action, a necessary practice for harmonious survival.

JUMPING REALITY STREAMS
At this particular time in scientific history, an interesting confluence is occurring. The smartest scientists are concluding that there are many more 'realities' than just this one we perceive. There are different methods of describing this new memory- including that we have reality bubbles and everything is made up of vibrating strings. It seems logical that the details of description will change as we perceive more information about the multiverse we inhabit, but one note will be mentioned here for more study. Scientist Dr. Michio Kaku (www.mkaku.org) speaks of the layers of cultural technology, and questions whether our human civilization will make it out of the most primitive layer (which we are in now), to be able to join the rest of the multiverse, and all the lifeforms that surround us. In the past, Animist cultures have been considered "primitive" by "civilized" monotheists,

but the most brilliant minds say that in order to move up to a level 1, 2 or 3 civilization (we are now a "0" civilization), we need to lay down some primitive methods and beliefs about how the world works, so we can evolve in ways that we are truly capable.

The worlds of science and spirit are blending, and scientists now admit that past judgments about what is "primitive", have been primitive. As Animists, our evolving intuitive and sensitive abilities are vital to our species' process of remembering our true capabilities. As we remember, we can ask to join in the conversation with the rest of the multiverse. As always, sensitive Animists will likely be the ones who receive the most important messages about where to be, when, to get where we want to go, or where we need to be.

May your sensitive nature always guide you
through the unforeseen dark holes.

SENSITIVE NECESSITY

Sensitive people have always been essential in Animist cultures. People who clearly hear the world speak can be incredibly important to the group at large. However, the common cultures of school or work do not publicly value these abilities. If someone hears 'voices' or sees things that others do not see, they can be looked at by many with fear, as a detriment, or a nuisance. Unfortunately, many sensitive people have been made to think that there is something wrong with the way they are. Now, scientists speak of Psychoneuroimmunology, the understanding that our thoughts have a relationship to our physical immune system. What we think about our experiences and "reality" itself, affects our body, mind and spirit, meaning that if we begin to believe we are sick and/or crazy, we can become just that.

Another side of this reality is that Animists are the ones who are time and space travelers, workers of the light and shadow, multidimensional communicators, and the spirit bridges for our future, whether we are unhoused, we live in a treehouse, a trailer or an apartment. As we remember our authentic self by listening to the spirits, trees and plants, we can shake off the sad, mean and arrogant attitudes of those who tricked us into disbelieving our own abilities.

Say the following statement as if you really mean it, or at least, that you really want it to be true... "I am sensitive and that is a good thing!" This is your most important tool needed to be able to find, recognize and use the other important tools you need for this work. It is also the exact way in which you have been made to most doubt yourself. The way unsensitive people control and bully sensitive people is to say "You are TOO sensitive" "your reality is not true" "don't trust your own experience" or "because you feel, see or understand this or that, you are CRAZY". After an entire lifetime, and multiple generations, of hearing this in so many ways, one begins to doubt their own reality. If you feel you are sensitive to energies, realities and understandings, claim it as one of your strengths and then learn to understand it!

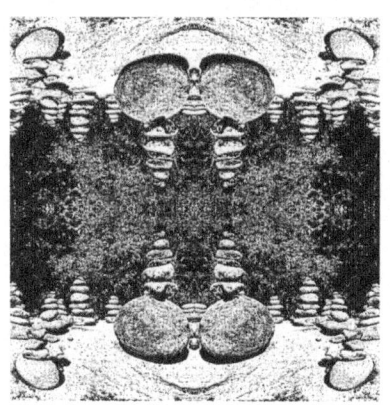

May the delicately stacked rocks
of reality ever be in your favor.

TRUST YOURSELF
It is a challenge, and an opportunity, to maneuver through the ebbs and eddies of the river of one's own reality, let alone finding others with

whom we have like mind. Many have been brought up under generations of trauma, despair and disbelief, and therefore most have many things to heal. However, only sensitive people will seek such healing. If you feel a desire to protect yourself from the meanness of emotional/physical toxicity, congratulations! You are sensitive! The wonderful thing about our times, is that there are many people realizing they are sensitive, and so there are many resources available to those ready and willing to unearth their gifts and integrate their mind/body/spirit. The living world needs each of us to commit to this process of healing, and to transmit the message "The world is alive, and we are a part of it!". Let this be your incentive to continue, when the unsensitive world starts to get you down. You are needed!

Your true test is if you can hold your own center even when everyone else around you believes something different. Each Animist must discern for themself when to compromise on an issue, or be willing to change an attitude, action or belief that fundamentally gets in their own way. One also must learn to trust one's own knowing, to decide when to leave, or join a situation, with another person, or vision of reality. Please remember, you are not alone, even when you feel you are alone.

As you read the following passages, know that making changes in your life is an intricate challenge, and we all have perceived limitations that we must learn to flow with, rather than get over. Here are a few self-care ideas as you walk your path. May they inspire your own ideas.

SELF CARE
Rest, personal healing, and self-compassion are all essential to the decolonization work that is a natural part of living as an Animist. Living in this culture is exhausting and traumatizing, and it has been all along. Each human has experienced pain and challenge, and more of us are looking for ways to find support in the healing process. Whether from addiction, trauma, neglect or self-doubt, each Animist is in healing-mode for multiple reasons. Trust your healing. Ask for help.

There is also a need for ancestral lineage healing and accountability, tracking injustices to make change, as well as feeling grief during this time of sickness and extinction. It is important to trust your need for self-care and mental health support. This work can happen in many ways but most importantly, what you do must help YOU.

INNOCULATE FOR DESPAIR
It is important to use your imagination to inoculate yourself against "fatal despair". For sensitive Animists, living in the ordinary mundane culture is harsh, depressing and mean. You cannot allow yourself to succumb to the ways of the cruel, so it is helpful to have a statement that you can say to yourself whenever you need it. Here is a suggestion: "I am 'in', but not 'of' the culture that is dangerous to me and mine" or "I trust that I reside in a beautiful and vibrant inner world!". Say these things to yourself often, and in your own way, and then make them true for you. By doing this, you separate yourself from identifying with, and being a victim of, the callousness of the ordinary world, and it aligns you with the beauty that exists around, and within you, at all times. No matter what the mundane world says or does, you are a part of the sacred web of life.

WEB MAINTENANCE
You are in charge of your own internal tech support. You must consistently monitor your energy, emotions and body systems to be as centered as possible at all times. Imagination can be a helpful tool for this important job.

Here is one simple idea to try.

Imagine your life, and your personal universe, as a web. Let your imagination flow about what it looks like, and how strong and beautiful it really is. See any negativity or scary things as food for your very special new crystalline spider ally, who comes to your web when you need help. Allow your inner knowing to show you any areas or strands of your web that need repair, for whatever reason. Spirit world journeying and energy medicine can help you learn to do this work yourself, and help you find assistance when you need it.

TOXIC DOSING
On every continent, when Animists were first exposed to the "People of Filth" (for many centuries, Europeans rarely bathed and lived in filthy, sickly conditions), many died immediately of horrible diseases they could not even imagine. Over time, a level of immunity builds in those who survive. Covid-19 has reminded us how a disease outbreak can run rampant in the general population, but other epidemics are now occurring in our society. Many people ingest poisons into themselves without even knowing it, in their food, air and water. High fructose

corn syrup (which is now called fructose or fructose syrup), sugar, alcohol and pharmaceutical medications are just a few. We cannot steer clear of all poisons, they are everywhere in our environment, but we can commit to our own self-care by not poisoning ourselves.

The Latin root of Hallucination means to "wander in the mind".

One way that the unsensitive culture tries to desensitize those who hear the worlds is to diagnose and medicate. The common theory of those who have had the power to diagnose, is that if one hears voices, or senses "unseen" things, they are abnormal, and automatically need to be medicated.
As the author of this book I cannot diagnose anyone about what goes on in one's head, please consider the possibility that if you, or your loved one, hears voices (especially if they are not malevolent) or senses things, you may be a sensitive Animist in waiting. Attempt to communicate with the voices. Ask them "Who are you?" "What message do you have for me?" and treat them as if they are long lost friends who want to help you. See if your (or your loved one's) experience changes for the better. Seek out someone who is experienced in such communication (use search keywords such as 'medium', 'channel', 'shamanic practitioner', 'intuitive', 'empath') to find written resources, videos, or someone to consult in your area.

POWER DOWN
For people of all Animist ways, we find ourselves in a technologically changing world, and so we need to adapt. Radio frequency (RF) energy waves from cell phones and wireless internet have enveloped most houses, neighborhoods and entire cities. The long-term effect of living in such waves is yet to be seen, especially for children. Since this is a growing reality, we need to take time out and turn off as many waves as possible. In addition, the more sensitive you become, the more you will notice how your energy is affected by, and affects, your technology. This means that your electronic devices often mirror your emotional and psychic bodies. If, or when, you get angry, tired, frustrated, hungry or sad, you may find that your electronics act out too. We all share energy with everyone, and everything, all the time. For anyone on this path, it is important to protect and rejuvenate ourselves. It is also important that we unplug, power down and tune out, to tune in to the subtle voices of the living world around us, as well as our inner worlds of intuition and dreams.

May time smooth your rough edges like water
transforming Tree to Driftwood.

A PERSONAL PATH

Animistic experiences are incredibly personal ones. You cannot simply read about an experience to know it. You learn through doing it, whatever "it" is. The Animist path is about aligning your energies so that you become able to hear the benevolent world around and within you.

We are naturally communal creatures, so it is important to acknowledge that when you hear a tree talk, or see a plant dance, you may want to share the experience with another human. However, the person with whom you share may not appreciate, or even believe, you. If you are with someone else at the time of the experience, your companion may agree with what you saw/experienced, and they may not. As an Animistic person, you must learn how to satisfy yourself with your own experiences, until you find others who can appreciate such realities, and even have their own to share with you.

A bit of advice...when a tree, plant or spirit wants to share something with you, if you try to share it with someone else and they don't appreciate it or believe it, don't be sad or upset. Instead, remember two things- first, maybe the spirit wants the experience to be just between the two of you, and second, maybe you don't have that much in common with the person to whom you just told something you find to be special. Maybe next time something special occurs, you won't share it with them.

Living an Animist life in this culture, at this time, can be a relatively solitary one. While you may be surrounded by other people, those with whom you can share this side of life, might be only a few. Even if at this point in your path you have no one else to share it with, do not doubt! Share it with your emerging living world, and you will not feel alone. As your connections strengthen, you will find others with whom to share your new life.

PLANT TEACHERS
Humans, and other animals, rely on plants of this Earth for nourishment and medicine. We have sought out medicinal plants when we need their help since the beginning of human time. The plants we absorb into our bodies (both internally and externally) are nourishers, teachers and healers and it is wise for us to honor the depths of wisdom, physical assistance and soul support that they have offered Earth. Life as we know it on Earth would cease without plants.

May the medicinal nature of plants
reveal themselves to you.

"Plants have guided me in ways that no human could. I owe everything good in my life to my experiences with teachers in plant forms." (2021)

For those who commune with, and are patients of, mood soothing and visionary plants, deep calm, helpful answers and healing are offered from the rooted ones. Animist understanding knows that all plants have their own life force, individually, and as a collective. Visionary plants are known to reflect our beauty and disharmony back to us and show us another perspective. They also bring up what is ready to change for our healing…emotions, traumas and pains, as this is part of their gift to us. The process of working with these gifts is an intricate initiation filled with potential danger ("bad" experiences and death), "bad" leadership (predation and appropriation) and risky outcomes without supportive guidance, so proceed carefully. Ask the plants to help guide you through the intricacies of communing with them. Caution is encouraged. Blessings are offered.

A female voice at the end of my first hallucinogenic experience said: "The purpose of visionary plants is to part the veil for you and show you where you can go…but you have to be able to get there on your own." (1994)

GENDER YOU

I wrote this chapter in 2010 at the age of 43 but neglected to include gender acceptance in this self-care manual. I added this section about gender in 2021 at the age of 53. Since before puberty I have felt not completely aligned with either of the binary genders, and as I have gotten older, and the culture has deepened its expansive gender awareness (now often called Queer), I have come home to my energetic in betweenness. I am grateful. I hope the same for you. I hold space for the healing and expansion of these aspects of you, wherever you are in the gender spectrum.

To be an Animist is to understand that gender is more than the colonized mind has taught us. Seek and find your multidimensional Self in all that you are. Your gender identity is yours to explore. Your body, sensuality and sexuality are yours to please. You Belong. Never doubt it. Gender acceptance helps all.

Know that in every culture we exist, and always have. Throughout human time we have played important roles in many areas of life. Often gender expansive people are healers, artists, and mediators between worlds. In some cultures we have been known by names such as "gatekeepers", because we have been the ones who have always tended the portals between the physical and spirit worlds. Our roles are valid in every society. We are needed.

*May the dew of awareness rest gently
upon your delicate new leaves.*

YOUR SPECIAL CHILD
If you care for a child who is having trouble in the world around them, or you, or their teacher is having trouble understanding what is happening with your child, then it is time for some changes. Please consider the following or adapt them to suit your needs.

-If your child indicates (openly or quietly) that they are gay, the best thing you can do is love and protect them. Help them find what they need to feel supported.

-If your child speaks of their gender as different than what you call them or what is on their birth certificate, please believe them and ask them about their experience and what they need. Find ways to support them.

-If your child shares that they hear, see or feel spirits, plants, animals, ancestors or 'others', set aside any resistance or doubt, and ask questions about what is happening, what is being said/shared (messages, visions, dreams, voices) and how they feel about it. When the child is ready, seek someone who can help them learn to interact directly with those whom they perceive.
When you decide to listen to, and honor, your child's experience, this will help them enhance their confidence and trust in self. When they have more confidence they can build a relationship with their authentic self, and those who are communicating with them.

Your child's vision or intuitive knowing, is generally not a 'hallucination' or 'delusion'. How you speak of, and react to, your child's experiences has everything to do with how your child deals with what is going on in their head, and therefore how they interact with the world around them. Until your child is a teenager and can find help on their own, it is your job to research and determine what is unfolding in your sensitive child. They need help navigating through this territory.

May you create an altar
for the blessings and harvests in your life.

AUTHENTIC, NOT APPROPRIATED
The name "Rhythms of Feather and Smoke" was chosen because it highlights three of the sacred inheritances that each Animist has the right to claim. For those who are not registered, or have an ancestral connection with, a particular Animist nation, you may feel that the rhythm of drum, the feathers of our bird friends and the smoke of helpful plants are not part of your sacred Animist heritage. Some feel that only some people can lay claim to these tools, and that if unaffiliated Animists use them, they are stealing, appropriating or copying from others. It is essential for recently awakened Animists to create a personal practice that is authentic, not appropriated from Indigenous or other traditional cultural arts.

A few ideas to remember as you create an authentic practice:
-Do not copy. Spiritual practice is art, and you cannot just copy something and claim it as your own. "Appreciating" is different than "appropriating" (taking).

-Explore your own ancestry and draw from these themes, tools and practices.

-Respect names that are specific such as "smudge", "medicine wheel" and "chakra" because other words can be used such as "smoke clearing", "4 directions" and "energy centers".

-Be careful to not overharvest living beings: 1) Burn cleansing plants in a ceramic or metal container, rather than an Abalone shell. 2) Burn widely available plants instead of White Sage.

-Do not take. Ask permission. Be humble.
Do not be defensive when an "oops" takes place. Apologize.

-On land and with People, wait to be invited. Honor "No". Do not ask for education.

-Listen for your own inner guidance.

May the rhythms of drum and rattle help you every day.

The Animist world is varied and diversely beautiful, and there are three consistent tools that assist the personal process of connecting with your living world: Rhythm, Feathers and Smoke.

RHYTHM

The rhythm of the sacred drum has been with humanity since we became humans. The rhythm of our Mother's heartbeat filled our ears before we entered this world, and our own heartbeat has been a constant companion, so the drum is a perfect way for you to stay connected with the multifaceted nature of Spirit within your body.

As the "Convert or Die" people invaded each Animist culture around the planet, one of the things they did was outlaw the drum. The drum was for communication between people and their sacred living world. This vital tool became a target, and anyone caught drumming was exterminated or punished harshly. This persecution pushed the drum underground, to wait until it was safe once more. There are many styles of drums, as well as an infinite number of rhythms, but if you want to see if a culture has Animist roots, look for a drum. Where you find a drum, you have found the Animist spirit, which is everywhere.

You too can reclaim the drum, rattle, or simply clapping your hands to feel your own rhythm. When you begin to play, you may experience feelings that surprise you, including nervousness (about how you are doing it, as well as if someone can hear you) and self-doubt ("I can't do this!"). Breathe through any feelings that make you want to stop. You do not have to learn or remember fancy rhythms. The "journey" drumming style is a consistent beat. Whether you play fast or slow, you may find that your arm gets tired, or your mind wanders so you break the beat. Breathe, center and start again.

Remembering how to make rhythm is a wonderfully meditative process that helps to free your Animist spirit so you can remember your natural rhythms and the rhythms of the world around you.

May you find a feather to mark an auspicious moment.
(These feathers are Turkey, found in White Mtns, AZ)

FEATHERS

Everyone loves a feather, especially Animists. For many, finding a feather is taken as a positive sign, a good omen for success. People have always loved to display and use the beautiful feathers of our Bird Brothers and Sisters in our regalia, our ceremonies, and for healing tools. They have been used as peace offerings, trade items and communication tools (between people of different cultures and languages, as well as between people and spirits) for thousands of years. Today, however, there are people who would kill a bird for money and sport so now there are rules to protect our feathered friends.

The Migratory Bird Treaty Act of 1918 makes it illegal for anyone who is not a registered member of an Indigenous community to take, *possess,* import, export, transport, sell, purchase, barter, or offer for sale any migratory bird, or the parts, nests, or eggs of such a bird except under the terms of a valid permit issued pursuant to Federal regulations. However, feathers that can be legally possessed include Duck, Pheasant, Grouse, Quail, Chicken, Bobwhite, Dove, Sparrow, Mute Swan, House Crow and most Pigeons.

Then, there are wild Turkey feathers. They are so beautiful, and legal for non-registered tribal members to possess. Turkey feathers are lovely, every bit as regal as an Eagle, Hawk or Owl feather, and they have also gone through a strange transformation. While wild Turkeys are smart and can take care of themselves, Turkeys have recently been domesticated, and often made fun of for their lack of intelligence.

Turkeys have been made "dull" by domestication, but they aren't inherently so. Find yourself a wild Turkey feather and use it proudly, knowing that, like many of us, they weren't always domesticated, they were dumbed down by their environment. Thank you Turkey!

SMOKE
People have always used the smoke of helpful plants. Where one lives determines which helpful plants to use. Many modern practitioners use the smoke of the White Sage plant, but there are countless others. Just a few names are Juniper, Cedar, Lavender and Rosemary. Each aromatic plant is medicinal in its own way and helpful to cleanse and purify both space and body. On the spiritual or Soul level, smoke is often considered the vehicle for the ascension of prayer to the realm of Spirit.

Over time, the plants themselves have always told Animists when and why to use them. There are many traditions surrounding plants, such as how to use them in a medicinal and ceremonial manner, and each Animist must commune with the helpful plants to know which ones they are to use, why, and when. It is also helpful to become familiar with the landscape in which the plant is found, to more clearly understand the wisdom of the plants who live there. Whichever plants you feel called to use, humbly ask for their teachings, learn how, when and where to gather or grow them, and show respect to them as you work with them.

One ancient use of the helpful smoke of plant allies is to keep infestations at bay*. Whether you have a musty smell, fleas, or bad spirits, the same plants that can assist us in prayer, can assist us in maintaining environmental cleanliness. For example, damp, moist climates have always been a perfect environment for mold, and trees like Cedars are infused with natural antifungal and antimicrobial aspects. For those who live in these regions, whether you live in a house, trailer or an apartment complex, consider gathering Cedar boughs and keeping them in your house and under your bed. Let them dry and carefully burn a sprig for their fragrance and aromatics.

For those in the high mountains and areas of Great Plains, consider using Artemisia Sage in the same manner. In the coastal regions where Bay Laurel grows, you might pick and use this plant for its sacred cleansing smoke. If you live in the hot and dry desert states, you must consider that mold can grow in swamp coolers each summer.

The smoke and leaves of the Juniper tree is a wonderful ally to help discourage the growth of "undesirables" in your house. When your environment is regularly cleansed of unhealthy growth, whether physical, emotional or psychic, it is easier to think clearly, and to focus, offer prayers for the highest good.

There are some environments where smoke is not appropriate, oils or sprays of helpful plants can be used instead.

Please do your own research about any plant you might use, and do so at your own risk.

May the smoke of sacred plants
cleanse and protect what is important.

THE TURNING OF HIS-STORY
"History" is written by the victors of each war, after they steal and burn the sacred remnants of the conquered culture. This has always been true, so when we desire to learn our fabulously rich Animist history in all its diversity, we often find very little that is written with an Animist voice. Many Animist cultures were "studied" by early European and American anthropologists as the cultures were being inundated with colonized ideas. Many anthropologists, mostly Christian men, judged Animist lives with an attitude of superiority, by their monotheistic standard. During those scary times, too many good people of the world's Animist Peoples were beaten, stolen, tortured and killed for wanting to hold on to their trusted ways, lands and resources.

While the whitewashed textbooks do not often state this, ancient Europeans were dominated in these same ways, before "Europe" existed. For thousands of years before monotheistic religions were created, the continent consisted of communities of People with various languages and customs, yet they were all who we would consider to be Animists. When Christians showed up and told the People, "Convert or Die", they perpetuated horrible things against the populations to make them comply. After honing their methods for generations, monotheistic colonizers, and their thugs, perpetuated the same sickness against Animist People all over the planet.

So, here we are in the unfolding present. It is time that we take control of our destiny, with the power of new communication tools, and the freedom to speak of such things without being taken away in the night (at least at the moment of writing these words). There are many Animist views of history that children do not learn in history classes, yet any of us can now research to find out these stories, as sad and angering as they are. We must question whitewashed history, so that we know what really has happened to bring us here now.

YOUR STORY

An important story to consider re-interpreting is your own. Do not allow any mean spiritedness to take root and grow its poisonous fruit in your personal cultural story. Do not succumb to the nightmares of the people of meanness and sadness that have shaped all our pasts. These most recent ancestors were made mentally sick by the world they created for themselves, and we are all living out the consequences of their choices. Let your sensitivity and imagination teach you to reach back even farther, before monotheism existed, and ask those ancestors and guardians to help you maneuver through this crazed world. Animists have been here since the beginning of human time, and we will be here to help the clocks of the mundane world melt into the time of the flower, the tides and seasons once again.

We live in times that our ancestors could only imagine, and that which we now find commonplace would likely be considered the tools of magicians, sorcerers, star people or gods. In this way, none of us are completely traditional anymore. We are being asked by our Animist ancestors to blend the wisdom of the past with the tools of the modern world for our descendants.

May the written languages of Insects
kindly teach you always.

95%
Moving forward as a growing culture, we should be careful not to fall into a trap called Utopia. If we assume that those who practiced Animist ways were perfect, and that all Animists got along, and will once again get along beautifully forevermore… we have another thing coming. We are human. We fight, we disagree, and we can be mean and thoughtless. We best assume that this will always continue in one way or another. There are ways to work together well enough to heal our individual selves, and our cultures, in the direction of our desired reality.
No matter our spats or fights, we must acknowledge that for self-affirmed sensitive Animists, we have 95% in common. However, for all of us who are "like-minded", and all those who seem so different from us, we need to try our best to work together to alter the dangerous course we are on, even if we do not want to be side by side with each other. We can surely put aside our differences and do what needs to be done, together and separately. At any moment we may need to work with people with whom we don't agree on 95% of issues, because we have our humanity in common, as well as our desire for food, water and health, and that collective 5% is everything.

If we find that we truly cannot collect our energy to work towards a common good, then we will likely unfold a future that is bad for most of us here on this beautiful planet.

GOOD PASSING
As an Animist, one must acknowledge that each of us has the Nature given right to choose our end point for this life game. However, our growing Animist kindreds cannot afford to lose valuable sensitives, pagans, empaths, artists, gender expansive and BIPoC kin because of depression and fatal despair so often caused by being sensitive in this tragically unsensitive culture. We must stay strong, supple, and clear, and we must encourage other Animists to be as well as possible in each moment. We must let our helpful ancestors and allies come through while living on this beautiful, yet damaged, Earth. If, and when, you feel to be at the end of your life rope, meditate upon the idea of you being connected to so many other Animists, and that you are of service to the multiverse. Then ask your inner allies who you should reach out to in that moment. *Then, please, reach out to tell that person how you are feeling and ask for support.*

When it is your (and my) time to leave this plane existence, my prayer is that the passing is kind, gentle, and relieved from as much regret as possible. May you know that you are loved, and your life here has had meaning. When Nature calls us each home, may we enter into another life stream that is benevolent and where we can have a positive experience with like-minded friends and loved ones. May it be so.

YOU
Welcome to You, the first ancestor of your personal Kindred. As you claim your place in your new Animist Kindred, over time you will gain allies willing to help you understand your gifts and reframe the negativity in your past.

Many Animists wait for their Kindred to find and claim them. Please do not fall into this hole, because it keeps you waiting far too long. Know that you are the One your Kindred has been waiting for all time.

*This poem came through fully formed
in the weeks after my cousin's death in 2010.*

WE ARE THE ONES

We are the ones who remember the (ice) melt
long ago we read bones, and spirits we felt.
Since the time before time, our ancestors knew
the breath of the Spirit is in me, and in you.
We talk to the animals and listen to plants
We know life is synchronous, not simply chance.

We went underground to survive back then
but time now to thrive, we want an end
to this era of sadness, when fools are in charge.
But this too will pass, Earth's power is large.

The Peoples of Earth, for us to remember,
in the web of all life, we each are a member.
So come join the circle, and reclaim your role
to bring back the balance,
to remember you're whole.
Intuitive beings, forever, from birth.
This message we share, a teaching of worth.

A bear, a lichen, a river and human
All equal in power, when our prayer is in union.
The science of Spirit has now taken its stand
with spiraling snakes, and DNA strands.
Rainbow wisdom may call you, to circle together
to drum, and give thanks, where time is forever.

We are the Ones, the time is right now.
No need to wait longer, we will be shown how.

May the trunks of your Tree friends create beauty for your senses.

Augmented Reality-
You enhance your world
with your own mind!
Nature-
You communicate with the
living world around you!
Intuition-
Trust yourself and listen
within to be guided!
Meditation-
Calm your mind and body
with breath and intention!
Imagination-
Let your Nature take you
where it wants you to go!
Synchronicity-
You know it's working
when events come together!
Magic-
The world is alive and you
are a sacred part of it!

*A new green stalk will not grow faster if you pull on it,
so have patience that your path will unfold one step at a time.
(Quynn's dream 2013)*

**ANIMISM
The Earth is my Body
My Body is the Earth
We are All Sacred**

May the beautiful web gently hold
the sacred water, always.

RESTORING ANIMIST TIMELINES

**Vision for the Peoples of Earth...
Life is Brutal and Beautiful...
The Earth People who make it through
are stronger, individually and collectively...**

**The People of the Heavens
are simply one more People...
Inoculated from greed and separation...
The generations find our way...**

**Each one more capable
and healed than their parents.
It is we who do it Together.**

As always, the path into our collective future is being created moment by moment, by our actions. You and I have a role in this creation experience. We need help and guidance from our ancestors and allies who want us to be well in an equitable world.

It has been obvious to marginalized communities for as many generations have passed since colonization, that the dominant culture is cruel and unsustainable. The clarity of the response to Covid-19 shows how the systems of colonization, white, male, religious and human supremacy have caused sickness of mind, body and spirit in all humans, even those who do not recognize it in themselves. Even greater in importance is that these sicknesses have now tipped the balance in the ecosystems of Earth, toward devastation of that which we all depend.

On Earth today, depending on where each of us lives, we may, or may not, be hanged or burned for talking about, or experiencing, the practices shared here. However, the problems facing us as a species do, and will, bring out amazing, and scary, aspects of us as people. We are diving swiftly down a tunnel of initiation, and we do not know who will make it through, so how we navigate these waters is of upmost importance. There are things to learn, and things to do, as individuals and communities, and we are being guided. We must remember to trust this truth, especially when we forget.

In many countries around the world, vast numbers of species of other than human Kin are going extinct. Most human children live in toxic environments created by the adults of the world that soon will be dead. While some selfish elders may feel that "it will last as long as I do" (and it might), elders in Earth honoring communities are doing everything possible to tip the scale away from devastation of all that is important. Each adult must think about what legacy is being left to future generations, and then find and create ways to add to the movements of justice and prepare for what is coming.

It is easy to be confused and depressed about our current world because most of us know that it does not have to be this way. The era of Covid has shown us all that we can change when we must. We can change our world more quickly than we would have thought possible, so it is time to listen to what needs to be done for this generation and beyond.

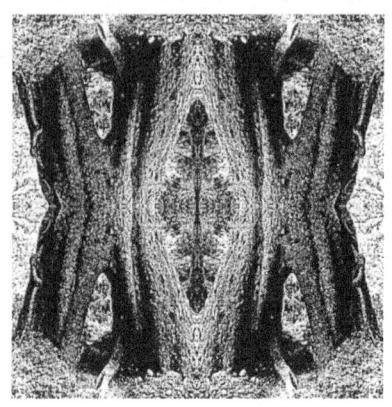

May the portals of the oldest Trees
assist in your ancestral healing.

Trigger Warning~
A COLONIZED VIEW OF THE WORLD

What must it have been like for Europeans after many generations of bloody crusades and horrifying plagues, surrounded by the torture of monotheism and the filth of their lives, who heard talk of a "new world"? Explorers spoke of a world that was abundant and supposedly theirs for the taking. At first telling, many must have thought it was a hoax or the drunken fantasy of a few sailors. Eventually there were those who decided to leave everything and go towards the setting sun, to hopefully find this "land of bounty" to the west. This paradise was a real place, but to the sickly and depressed people back in Europe, it might have sounded too good to be true, "Pure Fantasy!" some likely said.

Here is the problem… European Christians felt themselves superior to all who were not Christian when they sailed to each new (to them) continent. All of the many Peoples who had lived on the ancient lands for over a thousand generations experienced horrible cruelty and theft. All was done by the hands of the settlers who carried deadly beliefs, guns and bullets to back their endeavor. Superior technology was not to be denied. Another advantage of the Europeans was the sicknesses they carried, just by living the way they did. They infected entire continents with devastating diseases. They learned to use this technological advantage as a weapon as well. These events have unfolded in many places around this Earth for many centuries.

This is the history (his-story) that is trying to find healing and liberation now. The story behind this story is the dominance of Patriarchy, and that is an older tale. The thread that weaves through all these stories of dominance and cruelty could be called "soul sickness", the same trauma thread that now weaves all colonized humans together into an era of sickness.

SOUL SICKNESS

The Greeks had a name for such sickness, Miasma, or "spiritual pollution"- a highly contagious evil fate brought on by crimes against a mother or against the Mother Goddess's traditional law. (*The Woman's Encyclopedia of Myths and Secrets* by Barbara G. Walker, pg. 653)

If colonized humans are to address this cycle of pain, injustice, depression and a degraded environment, we must begin the healing process by first admitting that wrong has been, and continues to be, done. Many generations of kindred humans have endured much pain under these systems of oppression. To speak plainly, we must admit that these systems were created by those with colonized minds, so the solutions will come through those who still feel their connections with Earth and her kin. You are a part of the solution.

Pain continues to be inflicted now. However, there is a path out of this traumatic time in the human story. The beautiful Peoples of Earth need justice and equity, which promotes true healing. As more opportunities for personal and ancestral healing become accessible and available, our communities can begin to address the trauma that has occurred over many generations. As we go forward, we can apply personal healing models to cultural healing as well, because only a culture of healed individuals can become a healed culture. For those with European heritage, a key to healing is to be willing to think of oneself as a perpetrator, as well as a victim, of pain.

SIN= "TO MISS THE MARK"

This definition of "sin" belongs to the eldest branch of the Abrahamic religions, Judaism. Our Animist story began to change when the three religions of Abraham began to exert power in the world. What if the "original sin" (the ultimate mistake) of colonizing land and cultures of humanity, was when it was decided they/we had the right to take anything (land, culture, people) and kill everyone (human and non-human) if they/we wanted to, again and again?

The Christian holy book says the following: "If my people, which are called by my name, shall humble themselves, and pray, and seek my face, and turn from their wicked ways; then I will hear from heaven, and *will forgive their sin, and will heal their land.*" (emphasis added) (II Chronicles 7:14) What if the sin was that these ancestors went against the laws of the natural ways again and again? This verse reveals that even back then, the Christian deity knew that his people disrespected sacred lands and peoples.

The way forward towards is through acknowledgment, accountability and ultimately, hopefully, forgiveness. We must first admit that there is something profound that must be addressed so that someday it can be forgiven. Once we admit this is needed, and we acknowledge our part in it, we can find the pathways to the new possibilities.

May the morning light stream beautifully upon you.

MOVING BEYOND CURRENT CHALLENGES

One of the Star Trek series tells a story of humans in our Earth "future". After a horrible apocalypse, Earthlings alleviated all suffering in 70 years, the lifetime of a human being. What if we could alleviate suffering, racial injustice and climate collapse from this planet? If this is possible, then we must be willing to let go of the comfortable edge to which we have been clinging, and trust that a new future is available - a future that is better than "pure fantasy". So, how do we do this? If each of us shows up, learns helpful skills, plugs in, asks questions, and is kindly fierce in defense of this Earth and her People, we have a peaceful chance.

It is also important for you to know that the world needs you to learn how to trust your abilities. Our kindred world needs a renaissance of Earth honoring people performing Animist ceremonies and sharing uplifting prayers in sacred ways. If you are using the Animist arts (as described in this field guide) for healing and exploration, in your justice activism, or you feel called to be an Animist practitioner in your community, you are a part of the remembering of sacred ways to be in service. Seek wisdom and ceremonial actions that are helpful to those with less access to power than you. Pay your blessings forward.

WE ALL BELONG
What is important now is to flow with the day to day changes, while helping to create a well world for future kindred of Earth. With the help of our ancestors and allies in all realms, we will be guided through these unprecedented times. Wise prophecies say when the children lose hope it means the "end times" are here. The children of the world *are* telling us the end times are here. But the end always leads to a new beginning. What that looks like, is up to us. May we heal, trust and choose actions that guide us towards wellness.

FIND US. JOIN US. BE WITH US.
We can only do this work together as a Kindred, wherever we are in the physical world. Web of Life Animist Church offers opportunities to experience Animist circles and ceremonies (online and in person) that help us all remember our natural connections. We can become kindred with our inner guidance system, our Animist ancestors and our Animist communities. We remember these practices to progress through our journey of this life. We practice reciprocal relationships with internal and external mentors and ancestors for greater wisdom, strength, and persistence in this sacred work. As our movement progresses, we learn how we need each other to steward our Earth and our community.

Love yourself. Protect other Beings. Trust your Kindred Spirit.

Welcome to this end!
You have traveled through the Beginner's Field Guide
to Full Circle Animism~
You are now in the Land of WE.

This field guide is designed to be used as a divination tool by opening to a page when you are looking for an answer. If you notice a typo, consider it a gift. All ideas in WE are Quynn Red Mountain's and are not specifically the beliefs of Web of Life Animist church or Earth Web Media.

To dive deeper,
explore Animist training opportunities.
weboflifeanimists.com/product-category/trainings/

May the sacred web of life
surround, guide and entice you.

A last minute message from a visionary heart:

As typical with humans, it can be a challenge to agree and work together. In recent years, specifically during Covid-19, a chasm of values and beliefs emerged within Earth honoring communities. Areas of health, vaccines, politics and personal vs collective care have separated us. As the decades pass these differences will either grow, or dissolve, depending on what happens. Part of "what happens" depends upon choices made in our communities.

Will we agree how, and act to stave off white supremacy, fascism and climate collapse? We shall see. Will we be compelled to see each other as "WE", rather than "Me/Us" and "Them"? We shall see.
We all hover on the edge of Beneficial Change,
or Deep Catastrophe for all.
Which way we go depends on us.

Only "WE" can find our way
through this challenge.

**As a parting gift, use the coupon code "we"
for 50% off any purchase of courses
listed in this book**

Quynn Red Mountain
is an ordained Minister, Pastoral Counselor
and Spirit Bridge Practitioner through
Web of Life Animist church,
as well as a media producer and author of Animist content.

Get to know Quynn at www.quynn.com ,
in YouTube (Quynn Red Mountain) and in IG.

May our kind paths cross in helpful ways.

May you be blessed from the River to the Sky.

As we part ways, I would like to share something with you. After I was hit on the head all those years ago I received many downloads, but I also felt an impending doom for the first time in my life that I could not logically explain. The feeling was specifically worrisome, and there was a message with it. It said "If you speak of the things coming into your head, if you even keep thinking them, 'they' will come in the night and take you away." I had to push my way through this anxiety for two decades to keep going, always wondering who "they" were.

In the last few years, as the white supremacist fascists began to openly rear their heads, it became clear to me who "they" are, and strangely, that eased my anxiety about sharing the messages and ideas in this book. Now I know that yes, I may be "taken out" for speaking and acting, so please know that this book contains the essence of what was shared with me so far (minus some prophecies I will share later), and I now share all this with you. After I am gone, these are the channeled bones with which you can cobble together a new path for yourselves.

I was told in a journey once that Animists are like Rabbits, "they" might be able to kill some of us, but they will never be able to kill all of us, so may we multiply into the future. Thank you for reading, and doing, and being. Carry on and may good luck ever be in your favor!

May we always be protected.
Always.

Made in the USA
Coppell, TX
17 January 2023